THE GEORGE RODRIGUE
FOUNDATION OF THE ARTS AND
THE LOUISIANA RESTAURANT ASSOCIATION
EDUCATION FOUNDATION

WOULD LIKE TO EXPRESS THEIR APPRECIATION TO
THE FOLLOWING SPONSORS:

COOKBOOK SPONSOR

RECIPE SPONSOR

INGREDIENT SPONSOR

THEIR SUPPORT HAS MADE THIS PUBLICATION POSSIBLE.

THE POT &
THE PALETTE
COOKBOOK

MORE THAN 100 RECIPES FROM LOUISIANA'S GREATEST RESTAURANTS
WITH ARTWORK BY LOUISIANA'S MOST TALENTED STUDENT ARTISTS

FOREWORD BY EMERIL LAGASSE

FOR THE BENEFIT OF THE
LOUISIANA RESTAURANT ASSOCIATION EDUCATION FOUNDATION
& THE GEORGE RODRIGUE FOUNDATION OF THE ARTS

All proceeds from this book will directly benefit the programs of George Rodrigue Foundation of the Arts and the Louisiana Restaurant Association Education Foundation.

Published in 2013 by George Rodrigue Foundation of the Arts and
Louisiana Restaurant Association Education Foundation
Copyright © 2013 George Rodrigue Foundation of the Arts and
Louisiana Restaurant Association Education Foundation

ProStart® is a registered trademark of the National Restaurant Association Education Foundation.

All student artwork is copyright © 2013 by the individual artists; used by permission. Page 6: Emeril Lagasse with NOCCA students © Cheryl Gerber; page 7: 9 George Rodrigue with students and scholarship winners (3) © Geroge Rodrigue Foundation of the Arts; ; page 8: LRAEF competition photo © 2013 Jose L. Garcia, courtesy Louisiana Restaurant Association Education Foundation.

Cataloging-in-Publication Data has been applied for and may be obtained from the Library of Congress.

ISBN: 978-0-615-86341-2

Project Director: Marisa Bulzone
Designer: CThompsonDesigns, NYC
Production by Pamela Schechter

The text of this book was composed in Minion and Veneer.

Printed and bound in China, by QuaLibre Inc.

10 9 8 7 6 5 4 3 2 1

JOSCELYNE SILMON, *CHILDHOOD MEMORY*, **MIXED MEDIA**. (Artwork on frontispiece)

CONTENTS

A PLACE LIKE NO OTHER

Louisiana is a unique place. The culture, the arts, the music, the food—it's all a little bit different here. And we like it that way. Everywhere you look there's inspiration and creativity—from an unlikely soft shell crab dish at a restaurant to street music in Jackson Square to the way we're teaching our children in the classroom.

My longtime friend George Rodrigue knows this better than almost anyone. He has been a renowned Louisiana artist for decades; and now through his foundation, he's become a true educator and mentor. George has elicited the creative spark in so many young people. He believes in nurturing talent with a brush and canvas, much like I do with pots and pans. We both know that success in the arts starts with a vision, and we are so fortunate to have the distinctive Louisiana traditions as our platform. George supports teaching the arts to children and teens who otherwise would not have the opportunity to learn, which is much like the mission of my own foundation. These skills build confidence and can help improve many areas of a young person's life.

Our friends at the Louisiana Restaurant Association also know the value of sharing knowledge with the younger generation. The ProStart Program teaches high school students the restaurant business inside and out, especially the principles of hard work and hospitality for which our area is so famous. For many Louisiana students, a fruitful restaurant or hospitality career has been a dream since childhood. The Louisiana Restaurant Association ProStart program is expanding every year.

Much of Louisiana's rich heritage is captured in this cookbook, as this is an amazing combination of recipes from top professionals, brought to life through the artwork from our future leaders. I'm very impressed with the quality of artwork produced by students that accompanies the recipes. Through the work of George Rodrigue Foundation of the Arts, so many more students have been able to explore their talents, and to learn what it means to be a true artist. George has encouraged collaboration among all Louisiana creative disciplines, and I'm honored that he has placed the culinary arts alongside the visual arts for students to understand the breadth of artistic outlets available to them.

In Louisiana, we believe in supporting each other. George has supported the Emeril Lagasse Foundation for 10 years, and I am so proud of the many chefs and restaurateurs who have contributed recipes to make this book—which benefits both the George Rodrigue Foundation of the Arts and the Louisiana Restaurant Association Educational Foundation—a true reflection of today's Louisiana cuisine.

From Shreveport to Houma, Lake Charles to New Orleans, these recipes reflect the traditions and tastes that bring all Louisianans to the table. By passing on Louisiana customs to the next generation, we assure the preservation of our most treasured flavors, sights and sounds.

THE GEORGE RODRIGUE FOUNDATION OF THE ARTS

The George Rodrigue Foundation of the Arts (GRFA), founded in 2009 as a non-profit 501(c)(3) organization, advocates the importance of the arts in all aspects of education and life experience. Through programs such as George's Art Closet, providing art supplies for schools, Summer Art Camps and Art Therapy, as well as free lesson plans and a Student Art Gallery, GRFA encourages student, teacher, and parental arts advocacy and participation.

In addition, through its Print Donation Program, GRFA makes available to other non-profits original Blue Dog silkscreens, donated and signed by artist George Rodrigue. These prints raise funds not only for GRFA programs, but also more than $1.5 million for other non-profits, both throughout Louisiana and nationally, since the program's implementation in 2009.

In 2012, GRFA launched Louisiana A+ Schools, a research-based whole school arts-integrated network. The A+ model, with help from GRFA and the State of Louisiana, encourages creativity and stimulates learning by incorporating the arts into every school subject.

GRFA Art Scholarship Contest, now in its fourth year, has attracted almost 2,000 entries from nearly 150 Louisiana Cities. In total, $175,000 in scholarships and awards have been given to 67 winners. Each year's competition theme is determined by George Rodrigue and is announced in the beginning of the school year. In order to encourage participation by all, there is no GPA requirement and scholarship winners are not required to major in art. Artwork from the winners travels for public exhibition in varying locations, including the Governor's Mansion in Baton Rouge, the Masur Museum in Monroe, and the Ogden Museum of Southern Art in New Orleans.

Also, due to inadequate funding for supplies, many teachers and schools struggle to provide meaningful arts experiences for their students. By gathering donations of supplies and/or funds to purchase supplies through George's Art Closet, GRFA distributes art supplies to Louisiana art teachers and schools whose funding does not otherwise allow for the expense. Nearly

100 schools have shared in more than $130,000 in art supply awards.

Founded by Louisiana natives, artist George Rodrigue, and GRFA's Executive Director, Jacques Rodrigue, the foundation focuses primarily on Louisiana schools and arts education initiatives. However, George Rodrigue's fame, spawned by fifty years of Cajun folk life and Blue Dog paintings, combined with GRFA's increasing social media presence, encourages partnerships with schools and foundations nationwide, as GRFA attracts funding and awareness for its programs through a broader audience.

THE LOUISIANA RESTAURANT ASSOCIATION EDUCATION FOUNDATION

Since 1995, the Louisiana Restaurant Association Education Foundation (LRAEF) has operated as the official non-profit arm of Louisiana's Restaurant Association. Recognizing the unprecedented growth of the restaurant and hospitality industry, already the state's largest private employer, the LRAEF was created to address the growing need for highly trained employees and future industry leaders who can impact the direction and perception of the industry. As the philanthropic foundation of the LRA, the Education Foundation exists to enhance our community through expanded educational and career opportunities, the formation of strategic partnerships and the elevation of our professional standards and practices.

The LRAEF currently operates two signature programs. The first, a scholarship fund, grants one-time awards to candidates interested in pursuing post-secondary education in the culinary arts, hospitality and tourism management, or related fields. Since 2009, nearly $150,000 has been awarded. Second, the LRAEF operates ProStart®, a robust two-year culinary arts and restaurant management curriculum for high school juniors and seniors in Louisiana. The program is in nearly 50 schools around the state with more than 1,500 students.

These programs are focused on engaging and educating current high school and college students in the state of Louisiana on the restaurant and hospitality industries. We believe that our programs serve two primary functions: First, as Louisiana's largest private employer representing everyone from entrepreneurs and small businesses to multi-national corporations, with a projected increase in job opportunities numbering nearly 20,000 in the coming decade, it is essential that we provide support for the next generation of Louisianans to capitalize on the unprecedented career opportunities available in our industry. Second, food and hospitality are essential to our culture and identity as Louisianans. By teaching vital academic and life skills through this unique lens, we are better preparing Louisiana students for future success across all disciplines while simultaneously instilling practical expertise, self-sufficiency and state pride.

The LRAEF's work is based on our industry's distinctive profile of unlimited opportunity for growth, promotion and upward mobility, with little or no barrier for entry.

THE 2013 ART CONTEST

In 2012, the George Rodrigue Foundation of the Arts (GRFA) partnered with the Louisiana Restaurant Association Education Foundation (LRAEF) for the 2013 GRFA Scholarship Art Contest which was based upon the theme "Louisiana's Culinary Heritage." Both foundations are non-profit 501(c)3 organizations that share the same mission of youth development through the arts, whether visual, culinary, performance or other. And both agreed that a cookbook featuring selections from the contest artwork and recipes from Louisiana chefs would be a great way to fundraise and advance the mission of both organizations.

Once the first round judging was complete, GRFA notified the fifteen entrants with the highest scores and they were selected as finalists. The finalists, along with their families and art teachers, were invited to join George Rodrigue, the art contest sponsors, the LRAEF and the GRFA staff for an awards presentation and luncheon at the Sheraton Hotel in New Orleans on March 23, 2013. At the luncheon, a new group of judges comprised of arts specialists, chefs, and celebrities scored the finalists' original artwork in person based upon the same three categories as above.

After tabulating the scores, ten high school senior and five high school junior winners were announced and presented with scholarship awards valued at $6,000 for the first place, $5,500 for second place, $5,000 for third place; a total of $45,000 in scholarships was awarded.

Following the awards ceremony, GRFA, LRAEF and the cookbook's project director selected 35 additional pieces of artwork from other art contest entrants and past winners of the GRFA contest whose work best matched the recipes and theme of the cookbook. As a result of this effort, *The Pot & The Palette* cookbook was produced featuring recipes from many of the greatest restaurants in Louisiana and artwork by some of Louisiana's most talented student artists.

After a major media and public relations campaign, more than 600 students from across the state of Louisiana entered the contest by submitting a photo of their artwork online. Then, ten specialists in arts, museums and education conducted the first round of judging based upon three categories (interpretation of theme, originality, and overall design).

Thank you to everyone who made this cookbook possible! We are forever indebted to our sponsors (listed on page 1), our judges, the participating chefs and restaurants, and to every student and art teacher who took the time to participate in our contest this year.

We hope you enjoy and Bon Appetite!

CHAPTER ONE
APPETIZERS

Mandeville ★

SERVES 12 TO 16

2 (10-ounce) boxes chopped frozen spinach, cooked and well drained

½ white onion, chopped fine

½ stick of butter

1 (8-ounce) package cream cheese

1 (8-ounce) container sour cream

1 (13.75-ounce) can artichoke hearts or bottoms, cut in small pieces

¾ cup grated Parmesan cheese

½ teaspoon crushed red pepper flakes, or to taste

Salt and pepper to taste (go easy on the salt—the cheese is salty)

1 (8-ounce package) shredded Monterey Jack cheese

1 large bag hearty chips or crackers, for serving

BEST EVER SPINACH ARTICHOKE DIP
MANDEVILLE HIGH SCHOOL
CAROLYN SENAC, PROSTART INSTRUCTOR

Mandeville High School is a participant in the LRAEF's ProStart Program, a two-year culinary course for high school juniors and seniors. Carolyn Senac uses this recipe—which was brought in by a student many years ago—in class and also when entertaining at home. Feel free to substitute low-fat or fat-free cream cheese and sour cream in this recipe.

Preheat oven to 350°F.

Cook and drain the spinach. In a large sauté pan, sauté the onion in butter until translucent. Cut the cream cheese into small pieces and add to pan over low heat.

When the cream cheese has melted, add the sour cream, artichoke hearts, spinach, Parmesan cheese, pepper flakes, and salt and pepper.

Remove from the heat and pour into an oven-safe casserole dish. Top with the shredded cheese and heat in the oven until the top is brown and the dip is bubbling. Serve with chips or crackers.

HOT CRAB DIP
SLAP YA MAMA
WALKER & SONS, OWNERS

Ville Platte

Born in the Cajun town of Ville Platte, Anthony Walker developed Slap Ya Mama's signature Cajun seasoning while working in the family deli. He was looking for a seasoning with real Cajun pepper taste without all the salt of commercial brands. It's now a staple in many a Louisiana pantry and the company now makes a full line of Cajun food products.

Preheat oven to 350°F.

In a large mixing bowl, combine the crabmeat, cream cheese, cheddar cheese, onion, horseradish, mayonnaise, Worcestershire sauce, lemon juice, garlic powder, and Cajun seasoning until thoroughly mixed

Prepare an oven-proof casserole with cooking spray and fill with the crab dip. (You may also want to shake a little more Cajun Seasoning over the top!) Bake for about 30 minutes, until the top is nicely browned and the dip is bubbling. Serve with the crackers of your choice.

SERVES 10 TO 12

1 (16-ounce) container white Louisiana crabmeat

1 (8-ounce) package cream cheese, softened

1 (8-ounce) package shredded cheddar cheese

1 small onion, finely chopped

1 heaping teaspoon prepared horseradish

3 tablespoons mayonnaise

1 teaspoon Worcestershire sauce

3 tablespoons lemon juice

Pinch of garlic powder

Slap Ya Mama Cajun Seasoning, to taste

Crackers, for serving

BOUDREAUX ON HORSE-BACK (BACON-WRAPPED BOUDIN-STUFFED DATES)

JOLIE'S LOUISIANA BISTRO
MORGAN ANGELLE, EXECUTIVE CHEF

Lafayette
★

This farm-to-table restaurant is equally famous for its food and its art collection: named for George Rodrigue's classic painting Jolie Blonde, *its walls are also decorated with an impressive display of the artist's works. Equally classic are the menu's fresh interpretations of Creole foods, like this innovative use for the famous Acadian boudin sausage. This recipe is easily doubled or tripled to serve a crowd.*

Preheat the oven to 350°F.

Lay the bacon strips out on baking sheet and bake for approximately 6 minutes, till half-way done (don't let it crisp). Remove the bacon from the baking sheet and cool to room temperature.

Meanwhile, soak the dates in cool water for 5 to 10 minutes. This will make them slightly elastic so that they will not burst when you stuff them. Place warm boudin in a piping bag with no tip, or use a re-sealable storage bag with one of its bottom corners clipped off.

Remove the dates from the water and dry them slightly with a paper towel. Stuff each date with boudin, and wrap with 1 slice of bacon; secure by piercing a toothpick through each one.

Increase the oven to 450°F, place the dates on a baking sheet and roast for an additional 5 to 7 minutes. Serve hot.

SERVES ONE,
AS AN APPETIZER

6 strips bacon

6 dried dates
(pit removed)

1 cup boudin sausage meat
(casing removed), warmed

SHYANTHONY SYNIGAL, *A SLICE OF CULTURE,* OIL AND ACRYLIC (DETAIL)

New Orleans ★

FOR THE RICE

2 tablespoons olive oil

¼ cup chopped celery

¼ cup chopped onion

2 cups plain white rice

1 bay leaf

Salt, to taste

FOR THE STUFFING

3 tablespoons olive oil

2 cups chopped artichoke hearts

2 tablespoons chopped garlic

2 tablespoons finely diced lemon pickle

½ cup lightly toasted pine nuts

½ cup golden raisins, chopped

2 tablespoons lemon juice

3 tablespoons chopped dill

3 tablespoons chopped mint

3 tablespoons extra virgin olive oil

Salt, to taste

Crushed red pepper flakes, to taste

ARTICHOKE DOLMADES
BAYONA
SUSAN SPICER, CHEF/OWNER

The daughter of a naval officer, Chef Susan Spicer grew up traveling the world. Her international influences are shown in this flavorful take on the classic Greek appetizer, stuffed grape leaves. Look for grape leaves in the international foods section of the supermarket, or order them online.

Make the rice. Heat the oil in a pot or straight-sided sauté pan. Add the celery and onion and sweat for 5 minutes over medium heat. Stir in the rice, then add 2 cups water, the bay leaf and salt to taste. Bring to a boil, cover and cook over low heat or in the oven for 15 minutes. Remove from heat and let cool. Rice should still be a little firm.

Make the stuffing. Heat the olive oil in a pan and add the artichoke hearts. Stir and cook about 5 minutes, then add the garlic and cook 2 minutes more. Scrape into a large bowl and add the cooked rice, lemon pickle, pine nuts, raisins, lemon juice, dill, mint olive oil, and salt and crushed red pepper, to taste. Stir with a spatula and taste for seasoning. Adjust according to the chef's taste!

Make the grape leaves. Preheat the oven to 350°F. To roll the grape leaves, place each leaf on a flat surface, with the underside of the leaf facing you. Overlap the two bottom sections of the leaf, then place a spoonful of filling at the base. Begin to roll from the bottom, folding in the side sections as you go.

Arrange the rolls close together, seam-side down, in a rectangular baking pan or casserole. Drizzle with olive oil, white wine, and lemon juice and add water just to cover, then place a weight on top and bake for 25 to 30 minutes or until filling is completely cooked.

TRINITY HARTMAN, *THE HOLY TRINITY,* **MIXED MEDIA (FIRST PLACE SENIOR)**

THE SO-CALLED HOLY TRINITY of Cajun and Creole cooking consists of celery, onion, and bell pepper. These aromatics are roughly diced and used in the same way as a *mire poix* (celery, onion, and carrot) in traditional French cuisine—they are added early in the cooking and meant to break down within the dish, leaving only their flavor behind.

FOR THE GRAPE LEAVES

1 (8-ounce) jar grape leaves, blanched in water and stems removed

¼ cup olive oil

¼ cup white wine

3 tablespoons lemon juice

OYSTERS ON THE HALF SHELL R'EVOLUTION STYLE
RESTAURANT R'EVOLUTION
JOHN FOLSE AND RICK TRAMONTO, CHEFS AND CO-OWNERS

New Orleans
★

Named one of the best new restaurants in the South by Condé Nast Traveler, Restaurant R'Evolution is a sophisticated partnership between James Beard award–winning chef Tramonto and celebrated native son Folse. Together, these kitchen masters serve traditional Creole cuisine elevated to new levels. Here are their classic oysters on the half shell served with a selection of four sauces. Note that the sauces should be made well ahead of serving time.

Place crushed ice at the bottom of a serving bowl. Arrange freshly shucked oysters on top of the ice. Top two oysters with 2 tablespoons Cucumber-Lemon Granité, two with Tangerine-Chile Salsa and serve two plain. Place the Cane-Vinegar Mignonette and Cocktail Sauce in small dishes in the center of oysters, then garnish with lemon wedge on a cocktail fork. Enjoy!

CUCUMBER-LEMON GRANITÉ

In a blender, purée the cucumber, lemon juice, celery, lemon zest, sugar, and salt until smooth. Strain mixture through a fine-mesh sieve; reserve the sauce and discard the solids. Adjust seasoning to taste using salt and pepper. Place in an air-tight container and freeze. To serve, scrape off granité with a fork as needed. Makes 1 cup.

TANGERINE-CHILE SALSA

Slice tangerine segments into four to six smaller segments. In a small mixing bowl, combine the tangerines and juice with the zest, jalapeño, Fresno chile, habanero, rice wine vinegar, red onion, and salt and allow to marinate for a minimum of 1 hour. When ready to serve, blend in the chopped cilantro. Spoon over fish or oyster and enjoy. Makes 1 cup.

KATHERINE BECQUET, *LITTLE DELIGHTS OF LOUISIANA*, WATERCOLOR

FOR THE OYSTERS

6 freshly shucked Gulf oysters

¼ pound crushed ice

1 lemon wedge

FOR THE CUCUMBER-LEMON GRANITÉ

½ cup coarsely chopped English cucumber, skin-on

1 teaspoon freshly squeezed lemon juice

½ cup coarsely chopped celery hearts

1 teaspoon grated lemon zest

1 teaspoon sugar

1 tablespoon minced mint leaves

Salt and black pepper

FOR THE TANGERINE-CHILE SALSA

½ cup tangerine segments and juice

Zest of 1 tangerine, grated

1 teaspoon minced jalapeño pepper

1 teaspoon minced red Fresno chile

(*Continued*)

CANE-VINEGAR MIGNONETTE

In a small mixing bowl, combine the cane vinegar, white wine vinegar, white wine, shallots, pepper, and salt, and mix well. Refrigerate overnight before serving. Makes 1 cup.

COCKTAIL SAUCE

In a small mixing bowl, whisk together the ketchup, chile sauce, shallots, horseradish, Worcestershire sauce, lemon zest and juice, hot sauce, parsley, and black pepper. Allow to infuse in refrigerator for a minimum of 6 hours before serving. Makes 1 cup.

½ teaspoon minced habanero pepper

1½ tablespoons seasoned rice wine vinegar

1½ tablespoons minced red onion

Pinch of salt

½ tablespoon chopped cilantro

FOR THE CANE-VINEGAR MIGNONETTE

¼ cup cane vinegar (*see Note, page 25*)

2 tablespoons white wine vinegar

½ cup dry white wine

1 tablespoon minced shallots

1 teaspoon black pepper

Pinch of salt

FOR THE COCKTAIL SAUCE

¾ cup ketchup

¼ cup chile sauce

1 tablespoon minced shallots

1 tablespoon Atomic extra hot horseradish

1 tablespoon Worcestershire sauce

1 teaspoon grated lemon zest

1 teaspoon lemon juice

1 teaspoon Louisiana hot sauce

1 teaspoon chopped parsley

Pinch of black pepper

New Orleans

1 tablespoon vegetable oil

⅔ cup finely chopped button mushrooms

4 tablespoons unsalted butter

½ teaspoon minced garlic

2 tablespoons finely chopped shallots

½ pound cooked shrimp, finely diced

1 tablespoon all-purpose flour

½ cup brandy

½ cup heavy cream

1 teaspoon ground white pepper

4 tablespoons bread-crumbs

¼ cup finely chopped flat-leaf parsley

1 teaspoon sea salt

freshly ground black pepper to taste

½ teaspoon cayenne pepper

2 dozen Louisiana Gulf Oysters, shucked (reserve the flat sides of the shells)

Lemon wedges, for serving

OYSTERS BIENVILLE
ARNAUD'S RESTAURANT
TOMMY DIGIOVANNI, CHEF DE CUISINE

Oysters Bienville was created at Arnaud's, a restaurant that's been family owned and operated since 1918. According to co-proprietor Katy Casbarian, it takes it name from the restaurant's location at 813 Rue Bienville, which in turn was named for the founder of New Orleans, Jean Baptiste le Moyne, Sieur de Bienville, governor of original French Colony. This dish may be found on their à la carte menu as an appetizer as well as on the menu of their casual sister restaurant, Rèmoulade.

In a large, heavy saucepan, warm the vegetable oil and sauté the chopped mushrooms for about 4 minutes, stirring. Remove from the pan with a slotted spoon, press with another spoon to remove excess liquid and set aside.

In the same pan, melt the butter over low heat and sauté the garlic and shallots for about 3 minutes, stirring frequently, until softened. Add the diced shrimp and stir to mix, then sprinkle evenly with the flour. Stir together, add reserved mushrooms and increase heat to medium.

Stirring constantly, deglaze the pan with the brandy. Stir in the cream and the white pepper and cook for 2 to 3 minutes, until smooth. Stir in the breadcrumbs, parsley, salt, a touch of black pepper and the cayenne to reach a soft, pliable consistency. A small amount of milk may be added if the mixture is too thick.

Remove the pan from the heat and transfer the mixture to a glass or ceramic bowl. Cool to room temperature, then refrigerate for about ½ hour, or until thoroughly chilled.

Preheat the oven to 400°F. Wash the oyster shells well and pat dry. Drain the oysters and place one in each of the 24 shells, or use 2 smaller oysters per shell if necessary. Place the shells in a large, heavy roasting pan lined with a ½-inch layer of rock salt, or place 6 filled oyster shells in each of 4 pie pans lined with rock salt.

Top each oyster with 1 generous tablespoon of the Bienville mix and bake for 15 to 18 minutes, or until nicely browned. The shells will be extremely hot. Carefully place 6 oysters on each hot dinner plate. If baked in pie pans of rock salt, place each pan on a dinner plate. Serve with a lemon wedge.

OYSTERS WEEMO
WATERFRONT GRILL
DON, SAM, AND CLAY WEEMS, OWNERS

Family owned and operated, this restaurant is as well known for its beautiful waterfront view of the Bayou DeSiard as it is for its fine food. Housed in a 1930s building that once featured a glass-bottom dance floor and played host to such legends as Tommy Dorsey and Glen Miller, the restaurant today features a family atmosphere.

Preheat the oven to 375°F.

Assemble the oysters in their shells in a sided baking pan lined with rock salt. Pour the butter evenly over the oysters and sprinkle with Cajun seasoning. Add the mushrooms and chives in an even layer and bake for 10 minutes or until mixture is bubbling. Remove from oven.

Increase the oven temperature to broil. Top the oyster mixture with Parmesan and breadcrumbs. Return to oven and broil until the top is browned, about 2 minutes. Garnish with lemon zest. Serve with French bread.

MADISON BRENNAN, *GULF ON THE HALFSHELL (2),* OIL AND ACRYLIC

Monroe

SERVES 2

1 dozen raw Louisiana Gulf oysters on the half shell

Rock salt

3 ounces unsalted butter, melted

Cajun seasoning, to taste

½ cup sliced white mushrooms

¼ cup chopped fresh chives

¼ cup shredded Parmesan cheese

¼ cup Italian breadcrumbs

Finely julienned lemon zest, for garnish

Crusty French bread, for serving

Shreveport
★

SERVES 4

FOR THE SPINACH AND TASSO:

3 tablespoons olive oil

¼ cup diced white onion

2 cloves garlic, minced

1 bay leaf

¼ cup diced tasso ham

Salt and black pepper to taste

½ pound fresh spinach

1 cup heavy cream

Pinch of nutmeg

½ cup grated Parmesan cheese

FOR THE OYSTERS:

2 dozen Louisiana Gulf oysters

Rock salt as needed

½ cup panko breadcrumbs

Fresh lemon slices, for serving

ROASTED LOUISIANA GULF OYSTERS WITH SPINACH AND TASSO

BELLA FRESCA

WESTON MCELWEE, CHEF/CO-OWNER

Of this dish, which features tasso, the spicy, peppery smoked pork that is a south Louisiana specialty, Chef McElwee says: "We like to serve this dish in the winter months, and we really put a lot of effort into it. We make our own tasso ham in-house and I think that really boosts the quality of this preparation. You can certainly use any brand of tasso you like, or substitute bacon, salt pork, or even smoked sausage. Feel free to play around with different ingredients to make the recipe your own."

Heat the oil in a 4-quart pot. Once the oil shimmers in the light, add the onion, garlic, bay leaf, and tasso ham. Sprinkle salt and pepper in the pot according to your taste. Cook until the onions are translucent, and then add the spinach (a little bit of water in the pot will help steam the spinach). Once the spinach is cooked down, lift it from the pot (the onions and tasso should remain) and drain it thoroughly in a colander in your sink. Discard the bay leaf.

Meanwhile, add the cream and nutmeg to the pot and bring to a simmer. Add the drained spinach to the cream, and add the Parmesan as well. Cook until thickened then adjust seasoning with salt and pepper if needed.

Arrange the rock salt in a ½-inch layer on a rimmed baking sheet. Shuck the oysters and arrange them on the rock salt, as you would for an "on the half shell" preparation.

Preheat the oven to 400°F.

Place approximately 1 tablespoon of the spinach and tasso mixture on each oyster, then sprinkle them generously with the panko.

Roast the oysters in the oven for 8 to 10 minutes, until they are just cooked through and the breadcrumbs are toasted. Serve with fresh lemon slices.

ROCKIN' OYSTERS ROCKEFELLER
SLAP YA MAMA
WALKER & SONS, OWNERS

Here's a spiced up version of the classic New Orleans dish, this one courtesy of the Walker family. Originally created at the turn of the last century at Antoine's in New Orleans, the rich filling led to the association with John D. Rockefeller, who was the richest American at the time.

Clean the oysters and place them in a large stockpot. Pour in the beer and enough water to cover oysters; add 2 cloves of the garlic and season with Slap Ya Mama White Pepper Blend to taste. Bring to a boil, then remove from heat, drain, and cool.

Once oysters are cooled, break off and discard the top shell. Arrange the oysters on a baking sheet.

Preheat the oven to 425°F.

Melt the butter in a saucepan over medium heat. Cook the onion and 1 crushed garlic clove in the butter until soft. Reduce heat to low, and stir in spinach, Monterey Jack, fontina, and mozzarella. Cook until cheese melts, stirring frequently. Stir in the milk, and season with Slap Ya Mama White Pepper Blend to taste.

Spoon the sauce over each oyster, just filling the shell, and sprinkle with breadcrumbs. Bake until golden and bubbly, 8 to 10 minutes.

Ville Platte

SERVES 16

48 fresh, unopened Louisiana Gulf oysters

1½ cups beer

3 cloves garlic, divided

Slap Ya Mama Cajun Seasoning (White Pepper Blend) to taste

½ cup (1 stick) butter

1 onion, chopped

1 (10-ounce) package frozen chopped spinach, thawed and drained

8 ounces shredded Monterey Jack cheese

8 ounces shredded fontina cheese

8 ounces shredded mozzarella cheese

½ cup milk

2 tablespoons fine bread-crumbs

New Orleans ★

SERVES 4

FOR THE GREEN TOMATO JAM:

1 teaspoon unsalted butter

1 shallot, finely diced

2 green tomatoes, cored and chopped

2 cups Karo corn syrup

Salt and freshly ground black pepper, to taste

FOR THE PORK BELLY:

1 quart plus 2 cups whiskey, divided

¼ cup kosher salt

1 cup dark brown sugar

½ pound pork belly

2 pounds charcoal

2 cups hickory chips, soaked in water and strained

1 onion, chopped

1 carrot, peeled and chopped

2 stalks celery, chopped

8 cloves garlic, peeled

8 cups pork or veal stock

2 (12-ounce) cans Steen's cane syrup (see Note)

Salt and freshly ground black pepper, to taste

STICKY PORK BELLY AND OYSTERS
COMMANDER'S PALACE
TORY MCPHAIL, EXECUTIVE CHEF

This rich combination of smoked and braised pork belly with fried oysters typifies the inventive fare Chef McPhail provides for one of New Orleans's most famous dining rooms. This recipe features oysters from P&J Oysters; located in the French Quarter since 1876, P&J is the oldest continually operating oyster dealer in the United States. Note that the pork belly is brined for two days before smoking and braising.

Make the green tomato jam. In a medium skillet over medium heat, melt the butter and sauté the shallots until translucent. Add the green tomatoes and sauté until tender, 2 to 3 minutes. Add the corn syrup and cane vinegar and reduce to jam consistency. Season with salt and black pepper to taste.

Brine the pork belly. In a large bowl combine 3 quarts of water with 1 quart of the whiskey, the salt, and brown sugar; whisk until salt and sugar dissolve. Place the pork belly in the brine and marinate in the refrigerator for 48 hours.

Pull the belly out of brine and pat dry. Using a sharp knife, score the fat side of the belly ¼-inch deep in diagonal lines in one direction. Rotate the belly and repeat across the first lines creating X markings.

Smoke the pork belly. Light the charcoal on the far side of a grill; once the coals are ashed over, add 1 cup of the soaked wood chips. Place the pork belly on the opposite far side of the grill and close for 1 hour. After 1 hour add the remaining chips to coals, rotate the pork belly 180 degrees, close the grill and smoke for 1 more hour.

Braise the pork belly. Preheat the oven to 300°F. In a deep baking dish mix the onion, carrot, celery, garlic, stock, 2 cups whiskey, cane syrup, and salt and pepper. Add the smoked pork belly, making sure to submerge it fully. Bake for 2 hours, or until fork tender. Remove from the oven and let cool in braising liquid. Once cool, remove the pork belly and cut it into four 2-ounce pieces and set it aside on a roasting pan.

Increase the oven to 350°F. Heat the braising liquid on the stovetop and reduce by half. Strain the liquid and reserve for glazing sauce. Place the pork belly in the oven until hot throughout. Once hot, glaze with reduced braising liquid, reserving some of the glaze for serving.

Make the oysters. Preheat a deep fryer to 350°F. Pass over oysters with fingers checking for any shells. In a mixing bowl, combine the masa, all-purpose flour, corn meal, and Creole seasoning; mix extremely well. Place the oysters in the flour mixture, tossing around to ensure they are fully covered in flour. Drop the oysters in the fryer for approximately 2 minutes. Drain on paper towels and season with a pinch more Creole seasoning.

To serve. Place hot pork belly on top of seasoned greens of your choice; glaze one more time. Place one oyster on top of the pork belly and one on the side and finish with green tomato jam.

Note: The Steen family has been making cane syrup (from 100-percent sugar cane) in Louisiana for more than 90 years. The fourth generation company also makes molasses and the only cane vinegar made in the United States. Look for their products in specialty shops or order online.

KAYLA MCMASTER, *GRANDMA'S COOKIN'*, PENCIL AND GRAPHITE

FOR THE OYSTERS:

Vegetable oil for frying

8 Louisiana P & J Oysters

1 cup masa flour

1 cup all-purpose flour

½ cup corn meal

½ cup Creole seasoning

Seasoned greens, for serving

Metairie ★

MAKES 20 TO 25 BEIGNETS

¼ cup diced celery

¼ cup diced red bell pepper

¼ cup diced green bell pepper

⅓ cup diced yellow onion

1 bunch green onion

4 cups all-purpose flour

3 tablespoons baking powder

2 (12-ounce) bottles Abita amber beer or your favorite beer

3 eggs, beaten

4 tablespoons dry shrimp boil

1 pound Louisiana crawfish tails

2 ounces bacon (optional)

Vegetable oil, for frying

CRAWFISH BEIGNETS
CAFÉ B RESTAURANT BY RALPH BRENNAN
CHRIS MONTERO, EXECUTIVE CHEF

Beignets are associated with New Orleans almost as frequently as the name Brennan. In this recipe, the "holy trinity" of Creole cooking—celery, bell pepper, and onion—is combined with crawfish to fill these deliciously quintessential fritters.

Finely dice the celery, green and red bell pepper, and yellow onion, and thinly slice the green onion.

Combine the flour and baking powder in a bowl and mix well. Whisk in the beer and then the eggs till slightly lumpy; stir in the shrimp boil. Fold in vegetables, crawfish, and bacon, if using. Allow the mixture to sit for a few minutes.

Heat vegetable oil to 350°F in a deep fryer. Working in batches, drop small spoonfuls into the oil and cook for 3 to 4 minutes, making sure to turn occasionally. Remove and let drain on paper towels.

CRAWFISH RÉMOULADE DEVILED EGGS
RALPH'S ON THE PARK
CHIP FLANAGAN, EXECUTIVE CHEF

Rémoulade sauce may be reached for more than mayonnaise in Louisiana, and that's a good choice, as this spicy sauce pairs perfectly with the state's abundant seafood. This take on deviled eggs is classic New Orleans, as one might expect from NOLA native Chip Flanagan.

Place the eggs in a saucepan and cover with cold water. Add a pinch of salt. Cook the eggs over high heat. As soon as the water boils, remove from the heat, and cover the pan. Let the eggs sit for 12 minutes, then add ice to stop the cooking.

Peel the eggs and bisect, separating the tops from the bottoms. Remove the yolks and place in a mixing bowl.

Set aside 24 whole crawfish tails and roughly chop the remaining tails. Add the chopped tails to the yolks. Add the rémoulade sauce, sour cream, chives, Sriracha, salt, and pepper to the bowl and stir to combine.

Fill each egg white half with the crawfish mixture. Each white should hold about 1 tablespoon of mixture. Top each deviled egg with a whole crawfish tail and ¼ teaspoon of caviar.

New Orleans

MAKES 24 DEVILED EGGS

1 dozen eggs

Pinch of salt

¾ pound Louisiana crawfish tails

3 tablespoons rémoulade sauce

1 tablespoon sour cream

2 tablespoons chives, thinly sliced

1 tablespoon Sriracha chili sauce

¼ teaspoon salt

Pinch of black pepper

2 tablespoons Petrossian caviar

Lake Charles ★

SERVES 6 AS AN APPETIZER

1 pound Louisiana jumbo lump crab

FOR THE RÉMOULADE SAUCE (SEE NOTE):

2 cloves garlic

1 teaspoon Dijon mustard

2 egg yolks

8 ounces extra virgin olive oil

3 tablespoons lemon juice

1 teaspoon salt

½ teaspoon freshly ground black pepper

2 anchovies, minced (optional)

2 shallots, minced

2 tablespoons capers, minced

¼ bunch parsley, minced

½ teaspoon Tabasco sauce

1 hard-cooked egg, finely diced

8 ounces baby field greens, washed and drained (optional)

CRABMEAT RÉMOULADE
LA TRUFFE SAUVAGE
MOHAMED CHETTOUH, CHEF

Rémoulade is one of the many sauces through which Louisiana shows her French heritage. Mayonnaise-based and here spiced with mustard and Tabasco, it's a delicious accompaniment to many foods and goes particularly well with fish.

Place the crab in a colander and submerge into an ice-water bath to rinse. Gently stir crab to wash, taking care not to allow ice to combine with crab. Drain, and rinse again with cold water if needed. Set the colander over a bowl to catch the draining water, pick and clean any shells from the crabmeat, and leave in refrigerator for 30 minutes.

Meanwhile, prepare the rémoulade sauce. In a food processor or blender, combine the garlic, mustard, and egg yolks. Purée until smooth, then slowly add the olive oil in a thin stream, only adding more as it is emulsified with the yolks. The mixture should thicken as you progress. Transfer the mixture to a mixing bowl, and add the lemon juice, salt, pepper, anchovies (if using), shallots, capers, parsley, Tabasco, and cooked egg. Stir until thoroughly incorporated.

Divide the greens between six appetizer plates or large martini glasses. Divide crabmeat evenly and top with a large spoonful of rèmoulade. Keep chilled until ready to serve.

Note: Rèmoulade sauce can be made in advance and will keep refrigerated for 3 days.

CRABMEAT MAISON
GALATOIRE'S BISTRO
KELLEY MCCANN, EXECUTIVE CHEF

This lovely crab salad has long been a specialty of the house at Galatoire's, one of New Orleans most storied restaurants, and is served at their Baton Rouge branch, Galatoire's Bistro as well.

Combine the egg yolks, vinegar, mustard, and lemon juice in a food processor and process for 2 minutes. With the processor running, add the oil slowly in a thin stream and process until emulsified. Remove to a mixing bowl and gently fold in the capers, scallions, and parsley. Season with salt and white pepper. Chill for 2 to 4 hours.

Just before serving, gently fold in the crabmeat, taking care not to break up the lumps. Divide the lettuce among six serving plates and top with a slice of tomato. Spoon the crab atop the tomato and serve.

Baton Rouge

SERVES 6

2 large egg yolks

2 tablespoons red wine vinegar

1 tablespoon Creole mustard

1 teaspoon fresh lemon juice

1 cup vegetable oil

¼ cup nonpareil capers, drained

¼ cup chopped scallions

1 tablespoon chopped curly parsley

Salt and freshly ground white pepper to taste

1 pound jumbo Louisiana lump crabmeat

1 small head of iceberg lettuce, washed, dried, and cut into ribbons

2 medium vine-ripened tomatoes, cored and cut into six 1-inch thick slices

Houma ★

FOR THE TOMATO CREAM SAUCE:

1 tablespoon chopped garlic

1 cup diced onions

2 (28-ounce) cans plum tomatoes

1 tablespoon chopped basil

1 teaspoon chopped thyme

1 teaspoon chopped fresh oregano

2 tablespoons chopped fresh parsley

½ cup heavy cream

Salt and pepper to taste

FOR THE BASIL AIOLI:

1 cup mayonnaise

1 tablespoon lemon juice

Zest of 1 lemon (2 to 3 teaspoons)

1 teaspoon salt

1 teaspoon pepper

½ cup basil leaves

SHRIMP CAKES WITH MUSHROOM SAUTÉ AND TOMATO CREAM SAUCE
CAFÉ DOMINIQUE
DONNA MALBROUGH, OWNER

With a bayou-side outdoor patio, Café Dominique offers white tablecloth dining in this southern Louisiana town and adds a continental flair to traditional Southern favorites. Here, shrimp cakes are served on a bed of sautéed mushrooms with basil aioli and tomato cream sauce.

Make the tomato cream sauce. In a large pot, sauté the garlic and onions until tender. Strain the plum tomatoes and reserve the juices. Add the plum tomatoes to the garlic and onions. Add the basil, thyme, oregano, and parsley. Simmer for 20 minutes. Add the cream and simmer for 5 minutes more. Lightly season with salt and pepper. Put in a blender or food processor and process till smooth.

Make the basil aioli. Add the mayonnaise, lemon juice, lemon zest, salt, pepper and basil leaves in a blender and pulse until smooth and completely combined. Set aside.

Make the mushrooms. Heat the oil in a sauté pan. Add the mushrooms and raddiccio, and season with salt and pepper to taste. Sauté until soft and set aside.

Make the shrimp cakes. Preheat the oven to 425°F. Heat the canola oil in a sauté pan and lightly sauté the peppers, onion, and garlic. When cool, add the sautéed vegetables to a mixing bowl with the finely chopped shrimp. Add the basil, salt, and pepper. Fold 1 cup of the panko into mixture. Form into 2-ounce, ½-inch thick patties. Pour the remaining panko into a shallow plate and coat the cakes on all sides. Pan sear in canola oil until lightly brown on both sides. Finish in the oven for an additional 4 minutes.

To serve: On a small rectangular or square plate, pour 1 tablespoon of tomato cream sauce, top with a teaspoon of mushroom sauté, top with a teaspoon of basil alioli. Stack 2 shrimp cakes directly on top of the sauce. Garnish with a sprig of rosemary.

FOR THE MUSHROOM SAUTÉ:

1 tablespoon canola oil

1 cup button mushrooms, sliced

2 tablespoons roughly chopped raddiccio

1 teaspoon salt

1 teaspoon pepper

FOR THE SHRIMP CAKES:

1 tablespoon canola oil

2 red bell peppers, chopped fine

2 green bell peppers, chopped fine

2 onions, chopped fine

2 tablespoons finely chopped garlic

5 pounds tiny (90/110) Louisiana shrimp, finely chopped

2 tablespoons finely chopped basil

1 tablespoon kosher salt

1 tablespoon black pepper

4 cups panko bread-crumbs, divided

Canola oil as need, for frying

Rosemary sprigs, for garnish

Lutcher ★

MAKES 8 CROQUETTES

FOR THE CROQUETTES:

1 small onion

3 stalks celery

½ green bell pepper, seeded

¼ cup fresh parsley

Pinch of dried basil-garlic seasoning

1 pound peeled, raw Louisiana shrimp

6 ounces Louisiana crabmeat

1 egg

1 cup breadcrumbs, divided

2 tablespoons flour

1½ tablespoons Tony Chachere's Original Creole Seasoning

1 tablespoon butter

1 tablespoon olive oil

FOR THE DIPPING SAUCE:

1 (1.25 ounce) packet spicy taco seasoning

8 ounces sour cream

SHRIMP CROQUETTES WITH SPICY DIPPING SAUCE
ST. JAMES CAREER AND TECHNOLOGY CENTER
CRISTINA O'BRIEN, PROSTART GRADUATE

Located in the St. James Parish, the Career and Technology Center is one of 50 high schools in Louisiana participating in the LRAEF ProStart program. Former student Cristina O'Brien says, "I chose my Shrimp Croquettes with Spicy Dipping Sauce recipe because for the first time I had made a recipe all by myself. This recipe was a combination of my hard work and my hope to win at my local church cook off. And in the end, I not only made a good recipe but I also won second place in the appetizers section of the cook off."

Place the onion, celery, bell pepper, parsley, and basil-garlic seasoning into a food processor, and process until the vegetables are minced. Remove the vegetables, and add the shrimp to the food processor; mince until the shrimp are the same size as the vegetable mixture.

Place the vegetables and shrimp in a large bowl and mix in the crab, egg, ¼ cup breadcrumbs, flour, and Tony's seasoning (add more if desired).

Roll the mixture into balls or flatten into patties. Once formed, roll to coat in the remaining breadcrumbs.

Heat the butter and oil in a frying pan and, working in batches, pan fry the croquettes for 3 minutes on each side, or simply brown them in the pan and finish off in a 350°F oven for 4 minutes.

SPICY DIPPING SAUCE
Mix the taco seasoning into the sour cream until well blended. For a less spicy flavor, add only half of the packet.

GARLIC CLOVE SHRIMP
BORGNE
JOHN BESH, OWNER/BRIAN LANDRY, EXECUTIVE CHEF

This restaurant's namesake, Lake Borgne, is close to Chefs Besh and Landry's hearts; both grew up fishing in the lagoon that now opens onto the Gulf of Mexico. Borgne's menu is reflective of coastal Louisiana cuisine, with a touch of Spanish flair. This dish is a great representative of Spanish-influenced Creole cuisine. Sizzling shrimp in spicy-garlic oil (gambas al ajillo) can be found on many tapas menus. This recipe adds a rich shrimp stock and dry sherry to make a Spanish version of traditional New Orleans–style BBQ shrimp.

Peel and de-vein the shrimp, leaving the tail on. Season the shrimp with the Creole seasoning and place in refrigerator. Place the shrimp shells in 1.5-quart saucepan, cover with a little more than 1 quart of water, and bring to a simmer. Allow shells to simmer for 30 to 45 minutes. Strain the stock and discard the shells.

In a separate 2-quart saucepan, heat 2 tablespoons of the olive oil and sweat the garlic and shallots for 2 to 3 minutes or until aromatic. Add the piquillo peppers, crushed red pepper, salt, sugar, and sherry. Allow contents to come to a boil and reduce by half.

Add shrimp stock and 1 cup of the olive oil to the pot and allow contents to simmer for 10 to 12 minutes, or until all flavors have had a chance to meld.

Heat the remaining 3 tablespoons of olive oil in a cast-iron skillet over medium-high heat. In small batches sear the shrimp on both sides until golden brown and just cooked through. Be careful not to overcook. Turn off the heat. Return all of the shrimp to the cast-iron skillet and pour the garlic shrimp sauce over the top. Garnish with fried garlic chips if desired. Serve directly from the skillet.

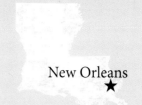

New Orleans

SERVES 8 TO 10

5 pounds jumbo (10/15) Louisiana shrimp, shell-on

3 tablespoons Creole seasoning

1 cup plus 5 tablespoons extra virgin olive oil, divided

¼ cup minced garlic

1 shallot, minced

¼ cup minced piquillo peppers

½ teaspoon crushed red pepper

½ tablespoon kosher salt

½ tablespoon sugar

1 cup dry sherry

1 quart strong shrimp stock

Fried garlic chips, optional, for garnish

New Orleans ★

SERVES 4

FOR THE SHRIMP:

For the BBQ Shrimp Compound Butter (see Notes):

1 pound butter, softened to room temperature

1 lemon, juiced (about 3 tablespoons) and zested (2 to 3 teaspoons)

2 tablespoons Worcestershire sauce

¼ cup roasted garlic (about 1 head of garlic, roasted, with the pulp squeezed out from the skin)

1½ tablespoons minced fresh rosemary

¼ cup Louisiana hot sauce (Crystal or Tabasco)

1 tablespoon freshly ground black pepper

Scant 2 teaspoons kosher salt

FOR THE COCONUT SLAW (SEE NOTES):

2 cups shredded Napa cabbage

1 cup shredded young coconut (fully thawed), or ¾ cup grated coconut

(*Continued*)

SHRIMP WEARING A GRASS SKIRT
SERENDIPITY RESTAURANT & BAR
CHRIS DEBARR, FORMER CHEF

According to Chef DeBarr, "This recipe has become a classic, playing on the flavors of New Orleans–style BBQ shrimp and Caribbean coconut shrimp—a nod to our tropical influences that takes the traditional dish on an exotic Tiki voyage! We roast spice-rubbed Gulf shrimp wrapped in delicate kataifi (shredded phyllo) and pineapple, and serve it on a tangy coconut slaw. Unlike the classic New Orleans dish, we can use less butter because kataifi captures the richness of the sauce but still allows for the savory, singing sweetness of the shrimp to shine through. Kataifi is the "grass skirt" that turns this into a playful, festive dish, and can be found in the freezer section of Middle Eastern grocery stores, or ordered online. For the home cook, it might make more sense to roast canned rings of pineapple, but it will taste better if you sacrifice a fresh, ripe pineapple."

Make the compound butter. Combine the butter, lemon juice and zest, Worcestershire sauce, garlic, rosemary, hot sauce, pepper, and salt in a mixing bowl. Beat with an electric mixer or a stand mixer fitted with the paddle attachment on low speed, until the liquids blend into the butter. Increase the speed to medium and beat until the garlic, zest and rosemary are evenly distributed.

Spread out four sheets of plastic wrap. Divide the butter evenly onto the plastic wrap sheets and roll into four logs. Freeze 3 of the logs for future use and refrigerate 1 log to use in this recipe.

Make the coconut slaw. Toss the shredded cabbage with the shredded coconut, coconut vinegar, ginger, salt, and lime juice. Marinate for 15 minutes. Add the coconut milk and toss. This slaw can be made 1 day ahead, and will last 3 days refrigerated.

Make the roasted pineapple. Preheat the oven to 400°F. In a bowl, toss the pineapple with 1 to 2 tablespoons of canola oil. Place the pineapple on a baking sheet pan covered with foil or parchment paper, leaving enough room on the pan for the wrapped shrimp.

Make the wrapped shrimp. Peel the shrimp, leaving the head and tail attached. Rub shrimp with K-Paul's Seafood Magic.

Wrap the seasoned shrimp with kataifi, approximately 1 "fluffy" tablespoon per shrimp. Set the wrapped shrimp on the sheet pan alongside the pineapple. Roast for 7 to 10 minutes, depending on your oven and the size of the shrimp. To check for doneness, test the back of the shrimp heads. With a gentle tug, the meat should pull away from the head.

While the shrimp and pineapple are roasting, place the refrigerated log of compound butter in a small skillet and heat, gently, over a low flame. When the shrimp are ready, increase the heat under the butter to medium and heat just until it sizzles.

To serve, divide the coconut slaw into four servings and arrange in the middle of the plates. Place three wedges of roasted pineapple on the slaw. Arrange four wrapped shrimp around the slaw. Spoon a little of the hot BBQ shrimp butter over each shrimp, and serve.

Notes: The compound butter quantity here is more than generous and can be cut in half, but it also freezes beautifully. Wrap segmented discs in plastic and freeze for future use.

We use frozen young coconut, which is juicier than the packaged, shredded coconut found in the baking aisle of most grocery stores. This quick-pickling technique brings out the fresh flavor. Coconut vinegar, a product of the Philippines, is rare but available in some Asian markets. You can also substitute cane vinegar. Look for it in Asian markets or order online.

½ cup coconut vinegar, or cane vinegar (see Note, page 25)

2 teaspoons ground ginger

2 teaspoons kosher salt

Juice of 1 lime (1 to 2 tablespoons)

½ (13.5-ounce) can coconut milk (approximately ½ cup)

FOR THE ROASTED PINEAPPLE:

1 fresh pineapple, trimmed and cut into 12 (1-inch by ½-inch) wedges, or 1 (20-ounce) can pineapple rings

Canola oil

FOR THE WRAPPED SHRIMP:

16 colossal (9/12 or larger) Louisiana shrimp (4 shrimp per serving)

2 tablespoons K-Paul's Seafood Magic, or other Creole seafood seasoning (but we swear by K-Paul's!)

¼ (1-pound) box of kataifi, thawed

New Iberia ★

SERVES 2

FOR THE MANGO SALSA:

2 fresh mangos

Zest (1 teaspoon) and juice of 1 lime (1 to 2 tablespoons)

½ red onion, roughly chopped

2 jalapeño peppers, seeded

¼ cup crushed tomatoes

1 tablespoon minced fresh garlic

1 teaspoon onion powder

1 teaspoon garlic powder

1 tablespoon kosher salt

1 teaspoon black pepper

1 teaspoon cumin

1 tablespoon chili powder

½ bunch fresh cilantro

1 tablespoon apple cider vinegar

SWEET POTATO BURRITOS WITH MANGO SALSA
CLEMENTINE RESTAURANT
BEN MONTGOMERY, EXECUTIVE CHEF

According to Chef Montgomery, this dish—created from the need for a unique vegetarian appetizer option—has become a house favorite of vegetarians and non-vegetarians alike. The restaurant is named for Clementine Hunter, owner Wayne Peltier's favorite artist. A folk artist, she was born in 1887 in the Cane River region of Louisiana.

Make the salsa. Peel and separate the meat of the mangos from the pit. Zest the lime and juice it. Combine the mangos, lime zest and juice, onion, jalapeños, tomatoes, garlic, onion powder, garlic powder, salt pepper, cumin chili powder, cilantro, and vinegar in a food processor and pulse until combined. (Don't over-process; the salsa should be chunky.)

Make the burritos. Preheat the oven to 350°F. Heat the butter in a sauté pan and add the onion and the peppers; sauté until soft. Lay out the tortillas and divide the vegetables between them; continue to fill the tortillas with the black beans, ½ cup of the cheddar, the sweet potato mash, and the blackening spice. Roll up the tortillas and place, seam-side down, in an oven-safe baking dish and top with the remaining cheddar. Bake for about 5 minutes, until the cheese has melted. Serve with sour cream and mango salsa.

MIRNA PINEDA, *PEPPERS,* PENCIL AND GRAPHITE (DETAIL)

FOR THE BURRITOS:

1 tablespoon butter

½ red onion, julienned

1 green bell pepper, julienned

1 red bell pepper, julienned

4 flour tortillas

1 cup shredded sharp cheddar cheese, divided

1 cup mashed sweet potatoes

¾ cup prepared black beans

1 tablespoon blackening spice

½ cup sour cream, for serving

1 cup mango salsa, for serving

New Orleans ★

MAKES 36 PIECES

2 stalks lemongrass

5 cloves garlic, whole

1 cup soy sauce

1 (3-inch) piece ginger, sliced

Juice of 1 lime (2 to 3 teaspoons)

½ cup salt

18 jumbo chicken wings, tips removed, cut into 2 sections

2 cups non-glutinous rice flour

Peanut oil for deep frying

¾ cup (6 ounces) jarred pepper jelly, melted, or sweet Thai chili sauce

1 tablespoon toasted sesame seeds, for serving

1 tablespoon chopped chives, for serving

"KFC" KOREAN FRIED CHICKEN WINGS

ROOT

PHILLIP LOPEZ, EXECUTIVE CHEF/OWNER

Local seasonal ingredients with global influences are the hallmarks of Chef Lopez's Root and Square Root restaurants. This is adapted from a recipe Chef Lopez contributed to Lorin Gaudin's New Orleans Chef's Table. *Melt the pepper jelly over low heat in a saucepan. Non-glutinous rice flour (joshinko) is less sticky than traditional rice flour (its name has nothing to do with gluten content) and can be found in Asian markets or online.*

Heat a large stockpot of water to a boil over high heat. Add the lemongrass, garlic, soy sauce, ginger, lime juice, and salt. Let boil for 5 to 8 minutes then turn down to a simmer. Add the chicken wings and blanch for 3 minutes only. (This will release some fat from the skin and make the skin tighter for frying.) Remove with a slotted spoon and shock in ice water. Tamp dry with paper towels.

Toss the wings in rice flour to coat well. Submerge wings, in batches, in hot oil at 350°F; fry until fully cooked inside, about 7 minutes. (Alternatively, place the wings on a baking sheet and roast in a 375°F oven for 15 to 20 minutes, rotating the pan halfway through.)

Place the hot wings in a large bowl and pour the melted pepper jelly over them. Stir to coat. Arrange wings on serving platter; sprinkle with the sesame seeds and chives.

VEAL MEATBALLS IN SPICY CHORIZO SAUCE
PAMPLONA TAPAS BAR AND RESTAURANT
KEVIN HAWKINS, EXECUTIVE CHEF

Lafayette
★

As its names suggests, Pamplona Tapas Bar brings a touch of Hemingway's Spain to the heart of Cajun country. This wonderful combination of veal meatballs in piquant sausage-laced sauce is typical of the small plates of the Basque region. Morcilla is a traditional Spanish blood sausage. This dish may be prepared and refrigerated up to six days ahead. Reheat over low heat or in a crockpot. The sauce can be refrigerated up to seven days. Chef Hawkins notes that this sauce makes an excellent marinade or sauce for pork; in fact, ground pork makes an excellent substitute for the veal here.

Make the sauce. Skin and mince the sausages. Heat the oil and sauté the chorizo and morcilla slowly for about 1 minute. Stir in the garlic and then add the tomato, piquillo peppers, coriander, cumin, paprika, and red pepper. Cover and simmer for 5 minutes. Transfer to a food processor and puree till as smooth as possible. With the motor running, thin out with a few tablespoons of water as needed to reach a sauce consistency. Taste and season with salt and pepper.

Make the meatballs. Combine the veal with 1 tablespoon of the white wine, egg, breadcrumbs, garlic, parsley, salt and pepper. Form into small balls (about 1½ inch). Heat the oil in a skillet and brown the meatballs on all sides. Add the prepared sauce and remaining wine and the chicken broth. Cover and simmer for 45 min, thinning with more chicken broth or water as needed.

SERVES 6

FOR THE SAUCE:

1 tablespoon olive oil

4 ounces chorizo sausage

2 ounces morcilla sausage

2 cloves garlic, minced

1 small tomato, peeled and chopped

2 piquillo peppers

1 teaspoon crushed coriander seed

½ teaspoon crushed cumin seed

¼ teaspoon sweet paprika

¼ teaspoon crushed red pepper

Salt and pepper, to taste

FOR THE MEATBALLS:

1 pound ground veal

4 tablespoons dry white wine, divided

1 egg, lightly beaten

3 tablespoons breadcrumbs

1 clove garlic, minced

1 tablespoon parsley

Kosher salt

Black pepper

2 tablespoons olive oil

4 tablespoons chicken broth

CHAPTER TWO
SOUPS AND SALADS

New Orleans ★

SERVES 12

FOR THE QUAIL:

12 boneless Bobwhite quail (see Note)

Salt and cracked black pepper, to taste

Granulated garlic, to taste

1½ cups cooked white rice

1 teaspoon gumbo filé powder

2 tablespoons chopped parsley

12 (⅛-inch) slices andouille sausage

12 Louisiana Gulf oysters, poached in their liquid

FOR THE GUMBO:

1 cup vegetable oil

1½ cups flour

2 cups diced onions

2 cups diced celery

1 cup diced green bell pepper

¼ cup minced garlic

1 cup sliced mushrooms

½ cup sliced tasso ham

3 quarts chicken stock

1 teaspoon thyme

(*Continued*)

DEATH BY GUMBO
RESTAURANT R'EVOLUTION
JOHN FOLSE, CHEF/CO-OWNER

Chef Folse created this gumbo for Craig Claiborne, the influential food critic of the New York Times. *He explains, "When he asked me to come to his home on Long Island to create a special dinner depicting the evolution of Cajun and Creole cuisine, I knew this unusual dish would be the perfect choice."*

Make the quail. Season the birds inside and out using salt, cracked black pepper, and granulated garlic. Season the cooked white rice to taste with salt, pepper, granulated garlic, gumbo filé powder, and chopped parsley. Stuff the cavity of each quail with 1 tablespoon of the rice mixture, 1 slice of andouille, 1 oyster, and a second tablespoon of rice mixture. Continue this process until all birds have been stuffed. Cover with plastic wrap and set aside.

Make the gumbo. In a 2-gallon stockpot, heat the oil over medium-high heat. Whisk in the flour, stirring constantly until a golden brown roux is achieved, about 20 minutes.

Add the onions, celery, bell peppers, and minced garlic. Sauté 3 to 5 minutes or until the vegetables are wilted. Stir in the mushrooms and tasso. Cook 3 minutes more then add the chicken stock, one ladle at a time, stirring constantly. Stir in the thyme, bring to a rolling boil, reduce to a simmer and cook 30 minutes.

Season to taste using salt, pepper, and granulated garlic. Place stuffed quail into gumbo and let it simmer for 30 minutes. When the quail are tender and the legs separate from body easily, remove the birds to a platter and keep warm. Strain all seasonings from the gumbo through a fine sieve and reserve the gumbo liquid. Return the liquid to the pot, add the quail, green onions, and parsley then bring to a low boil.

To serve, place 1 quail in center of each soup bowl and cover with gumbo liquid.

Note: Although it is best to use boneless quail for this recipe, you may also use bone-in birds if boneless are not available.

GUMBO IS THE BEST-KNOWN and most popular of all the dishes associated with Louisiana cuisine. Every family and restaurant has their own recipe (sometimes more than one), some with seafood, some with chicken and sausage, some with other ingredients entirely. The variety of Louisiana gumbo is reflected in a very small way on these pages.

Salt and cracked black pepper to taste

Granulated garlic to taste

12 stuffed and seasoned Bobwhite quail

1 cup sliced green onions

1 cup chopped parsley

ALFONSO VACA-LOYOLA, *THE CUTTING EDGE OF LOUISIANA FOODS*, OIL AND ACRYLIC

New Orleans

★

1 bunch mustard greens

1 bunch collard greens

1 bunch turnip greens

1 bunch watercress

1 bunch beet tops

1 bunch carrot tops

1 bunch spinach

½ head lettuce

½ head cabbage

2 medium onions, chopped (about 3 cups)

4 cloves garlic, crushed and chopped

5 tablespoons flour

1 pound smoked sausage

1 pound smoked ham

1 pound brisket

1 pound stew meat

1 pound chaurice hot sausage

1 teaspoon thyme leaves

1 teaspoon cayenne pepper

1 teaspoon gumbo filé powder

Steamed white rice for serving

LEAH CHASE'S GUMBO Z'HERBES
DOOKY CHASE'S RESTAURANT
LEAH CHASE, CHEF/OWNER

New Orleans is a city of traditions, and there's none more respected than a Holy Thursday after-mass visit to Dooky Chase's Restaurant for gumbo z'herbes. The legendary Leah Chase still presides over the kitchen at age 90, making gallons of this special gumbo on the day in question. Originally meatless in keeping with the custom of giving up meat for Lent, this version is rich with sausages, ham, and other meats. The (always odd for good luck) number of different greens is said to predict the number of friends the diner will make in the coming year. Ms. Chase's recipe features nine.

Clean the mustard, collard and turnip greens, watercress, beet and carrot tops, spinach, lettuce, and cabbage under cold running water, making sure to pick out any bad leaves and rinse away any grit. Chop coarsely and place in a 12-quart stockpot with the onions and garlic. Cover with water (about 1½ gallons), bring to a boil, reduce to a simmer, cover and cook for 30 minutes.

Strain the greens and reserve the liquid. Cut the smoked sausage, ham, brisket, and stew meat into bite-sized (about 1 inch) pieces and place in 12-quart stockpot with 2 cups of the reserved liquid. Steam over a high heat for 15 minutes.

Meanwhile cut the chaurice into bite-sized pieces and place in a skillet over high heat to render, about 10 minutes. Remove the chaurice, keeping the grease in the skillet, and set aside.

Blend the greens in a food processor until pureed. Heat the skillet of chaurice grease over a high heat and add flour. Cook roux until flour is cooked, about 5 minutes (it does not have to be brown). Pour the roux over the meat mixture and stir to combine.

Add pureed greens to the meat in the stockpot and add 2 quarts of the reserved liquid. Let simmer over a low heat for 20 minutes. Add the chaurice, thyme, and cayenne, and stir well. Season and simmer for 40 minutes more. Stir in the gumbo filé powder and remove from heat. Serve over steamed rice.

CREOLE OKRA SEAFOOD GUMBO

POPPY'S THE CRAZY LOBSTER BAR AND GRILL
A.J. TUSA, OWNER

Located on the banks of the Mississippi just outside the French Quarter, this lively seafood spot features live entertainment and a party atmosphere. This is owner A. J. "Poppy" Tusa's personal recipe.

Make a roux. In a medium saucepan, melt the butter, and slowly blend in the flour. Cook until a dark brown roux develops, about 45 minutes. Stir constantly so it doesn't burn. Remove from heat, and set aside until needed.

In a large sauté pan, heat ½ cup of the vegetable oil and sauté the okra until it begins to break and takes on a sticky consistently. Remove from heat, and set aside until needed.

In another large sauté pan, heat the remaining ½ cup of vegetable oil and sauté the onions, celery, and bell pepper until the onions are translucent. Remove from heat and set aside until needed.

Make shrimp stock. Peel and clean the shrimp, setting the peeled shrimp tails aside until needed. Now, take the heads and the shells and place in your favorite (10-quart) gumbo pot. Add 4 quarts of water, and boil for 15 minutes. Remove the heads and shells from the pot and discard.

Make the gumbo. Everything that was set aside until needed is now going to go to work. First, add your okra, sautéed vegetables, and the tomatoes to your gumbo pot, and season to your taste with salt, black pepper, and cayenne. Let boil for 15 minutes then turn off the heat, and slowly add your roux to the pot. As you add the roux you must whisk the pot constantly until you achieve the thickness that you desire (some people like thick, some people like thin).

Fire up the pot again, and boil for another 15 minutes, then reduce to a simmer. Add the shrimp and crab claw meat and simmer for 15 minutes more; then add your oysters and simmer for 5 minutes more. Finally, serve with white rice.

New Orleans ★

SERVES 10 TO 12

1 pound (4 sticks) butter

2 cups all-purpose flour

4 cups cut okra

1 cup vegetable oil, divided

2 cups chopped onion (2 medium onions)

1 ¼ cups chopped celery (2 stalks celery)

¾ cups chopped green bell pepper (1 medium pepper)

2 pounds large (31/35) Louisiana shrimp, unpeeled, heads on

4 cups diced tomatoes (about 2½ pounds)

Sea salt and freshly ground black pepper, to taste

Cayenne pepper, to taste

2 pounds Louisiana claw crabmeat

3 dozen Louisiana Gulf oysters, shucked

White rice, for serving

New Orleans ★

SEAFOOD GUMBO
NEW ORLEANS COUNTRY CLUB
CHRIS TEFARIKIS, EXECUTIVE CHEF

Catering to elegant affairs as well as hungry golfers, Chef Tefarikis is used to cooking for a crowd. This crabmeat gumbo recipe is great for large parties or even tailgating; it also freezes well.

FOR THE DARK ROUX:

2½ cups (5 sticks) butter

4½ cups all-purpose flour

FOR THE GUMBO:

½ cup vegetable oil

1 pound yellow onions, diced

1 pound celery, diced

1 pound green bell pepper, diced

1½ tablespoons thyme

3 tablespoons plus
1 teaspoon minced garlic

3 (14.5-ounce) cans diced tomatoes in juice

7 tablespoons Crystal hot sauce

4 gallons Seafood Gumbo Stock (*opposite*)

8 bay leaves,
boiled in water

1½ pounds Louisiana claw crabmeat

2½ pounds okra

Salt and pepper to taste

Cooked white rice for serving

Make the dark roux. In a large saucepan, melt the butter. When foaming, add the flour and stir to combine. Continue to cook over low heat, stirring frequently, until a dark (chocolate-colored) brown roux is achieved, about 45 minutes.

Add the vegetable oil to a very large stock pot; when heated, add the onions, celery, and bell pepper and sauté until the onions are transparent. Add the diced tomatoes and juice and 4 gallons of the seafood stock. Bring to a boil. Stir in the dark roux, let it return to a boil then reduce to a simmer. Skim any fat that may appear in the center as the gumbo is at strong simmer. Stir in the hot sauce, add the claw crabmeat and okra, and salt and pepper to taste.

To cool the gumbo for portioning, seal ice tightly in plastic bags and drop them in the pot, then place the pot in a sink full of ice water.

OLIVIA LOCASCIO, *PASS IT ON,* MIXED MEDIA

SEAFOOD GUMBO STOCK

Gumbo crabs are small Gulf Coast blue crabs. Use fresh or buy them frozen.

Rinse the fish bones under hot water then place in a large stock pot and bring to a boil; let boil for 10 minutes then strain and rinse the bones again. Return the bones to the pot and cover with 8 gallons fresh water. Add the onions, carrots, and celery, and let cook just below a simmer for 1 hour.

Preheat the oven to 400°F. Beat the crabs with a mallet and roast in the oven for 10 minutes. Add to the roasted crabs, white wine and peppercorns to the stock pot and then let stand again just below a simmer for 1 hour more. Strain then cool in an ice bath.

FOR THE SEAFOOD
GUMBO STOCK:

MAKES ABOUT 6 GALLONS

4 pounds fish bones
(no heads)

½ pound onions, chopped

¼ pound carrots, peeled
and chopped

¼ pound celery, chopped

6 pounds gumbo crabs

3½ tablespoons black
peppercorns

1½ cups white wine

CHICKEN AND SAUSAGE GUMBO

LES GUERIN, CHEF

Baton Rouge
★

A necessary ingredient in gumbo is the gumbo filé powder, which is made from the dried leaves of the sassafras, and will serve as a thickener. Look for it in the seasonings aisle of the supermarket, or order online.

Heat the oil in a saucepan and add the flour. Cook over low flame, stirring frequently, until a dark brown roux is formed, about 45 minutes.

Add the garlic, celery, onions, and bell pepper and set aside. In a skillet, fry the sliced sausage then add it to the roux-vegetable mixture. Pour 1 gallon of hot water and the Kitchen Bouquet into a large pot. Add the roux mixture, Worcestershire, gumbo filé, salt, and pepper. Bring to a boil and let it cook for about 20 minutes.

Meanwhile, brown the chicken. Add the chicken, parsley, and green onions to the pot and cook for 45 minutes more. Serve with rice.

SERVES 8 TO 10

1¾ cups vegetable oil

2½ cups flour

3 cloves garlic chopped

1 cup chopped celery

3 cups chopped onions

1½ cups chopped green bell pepper

2 pounds smoked sausage, sliced

3 tablespoons Kitchen Bouquet

2 tablespoons Worcestershire sauce

2 tablespoons gumbo filé powder

3 tablespoons salt

3 tablespoons freshly ground black pepper

4 pounds boneless chicken, cubed

1 cup chopped parsley

2 cups chopped green onions

10 cups cooked white rice, for serving

HAILEY DUPONT, *JEUNE FILLE DE FRUITS DE MER*, MIXED MEDIA (THIRD PLACE JUNIOR)

Shreveport

4 tomatoes, cut in half

2 red bell peppers, cut in half

¼ cup olive oil

2 large onions, cut in half with skin

6 cloves garlic

2 cucumbers, peeled and coarsely chopped

¼ cup red wine vinegar

¼ teaspoon salt

Blackened seasoning, to taste

¾ cup tomato juice

3 tablespoon Worcestershire sauce

½ teaspoon Tabasco sauce

2 tablespoons lemon or lime juice

1 tablespoon finely chopped cucumber, for garnish

1 tablespoon each of finely chopped red bell pepper, red onion, and fresh parsley, for garnish

GAZPACHO
THE SHREVEPORT CLUB
KEITH LENARD, EXECUTIVE CHEF

The Shreveport Club was formed in 1945 when a group of local businessmen gathered to create a private social club. In 1956, the club moved to its present home on Travis Street. Members and their guests can choose from a large selection of traditional Louisiana and continental fare.

Preheat oven to 350°F. De-stem and seed the tomatoes and the peppers; lightly coat in olive oil, then roast in the oven. Lightly coat the onions and roast in a separate pan. Roast or sauté the garlic in olive oil on the stove top just until brown.

Place the roasted tomatoes, pepper, onions, and garlic in a blender, and add the cucumber. Blend to combine.

Add the vinegar, salt, blackened seasoning, tomato juice, Worcestershire sauce, Tabasco, and lemon juice. Blend to combine then strain through a small or medium strainer. Taste and adjust seasoning to desired spiciness.

Garnish with the brunoise of cucumber, red pepper, red onion, and parsley.

POACHED GARLIC SOUP
THE SHREVEPORT CLUB
KEITH LENARD, EXECUTIVE CHEF

Don't let the poached garlic in this recipe go to waste. Use it to make toasted garlic bread.

In a medium saucepan over medium-high heat, combine garlic cloves and 3 cups of vegetable broth; bring to a boil and poach the garlic for 15 minutes or until soft. With a slotted spoon, remove the garlic cloves to a small bowl and mash with a fork; reserve for another use.

Continue to cook and reduce the broth to a glaze; remove from heat and set aside.

In a large soup pot over low heat, melt the butter. Add the onion and sauté until soft. Drain the water from the potatoes and stir them into the butter and onion mixture. Season with salt and pepper. Add the remaining 4 cups vegetable broth. Increase heat to medium-high; simmer, uncovered, 25 minutes or until the potatoes are softened. Remove from heat and let cool 10 to 15 minutes.

In a food processor or blender, puree the soup and then return it to the soup pot. Add the reserved glaze; stir until well blended. At this stage, the soup can be held in the refrigerator for 1 to 2 days in advance of serving.

To finish the soup, stir in the heavy cream, milk, salt, and pepper; cook, over low heat, another 10 minutes. Serve in soup bowls and garnish with Parmesan cheese.

Shreveport

SERVES 6

30 cloves garlic, peeled

7 cups good-quality vegetable or chicken broth, divided

½ cup (1 stick) butter

½ cup chopped white onion

8 small new potatoes, peeled, diced, and reserved in cold water

Salt and pepper, to taste

1 cup heavy cream

1 cup milk

Coarse salt and freshly cracked pepper, to taste

Freshly grated Parmesan cheese, for serving

Lake Charles
★

SERVES 8 TO 10

6 fluid ounces clarified butter (or vegetable oil)

5 pounds yellow or sweet onions, sliced

4 cloves garlic, minced

¼ cup all-purpose flour

3 quarts rich beef or chicken stock

1 cup port wine

1 cup red wine

3 bay leaves

2 teaspoons peppercorns

3 sprigs thyme

Small bunch of fresh parsley

2 tablespoons sea salt

1 tablespoon freshly ground black pepper

1 baguette, sliced and toasted

6 ounces Gruyère cheese

FRENCH ONION SOUP
LA TRUFFE SAUVAGE
MOHAMED CHETTOUH, CHEF

A staple at "The Wild Truffle" since the restaurant opened in 1998, Chef Chettouh says that the key is careful browning of the onions, which requires attention and regular stirring. Don't be intimidated by the amount of onions at first, they cook down quite a bit. This soup can be made in advance and freezes well.

Heat a heavy bottom stock pot until quite hot, then add the butter and onions. Stir at intervals, allowing the onions to brown nicely. The key to onion soup is browning the onions well without scorching. Stir as needed, and lower the heat so the onions will brown instead of burn.

When the onions have cooked down, and have taken on a nice brown color, add the garlic and continue to cook until the garlic is browned but not burnt. Add the flour, stir well throughout and cook briefly; the mixture will become thick. Add the stock, port, and red wine. Bring to a boil, skimming the foam as it approaches boiling.

Preheat the oven to 400°F.

Make a bouquet garni by wrapping the bay leaves, peppercorns, thyme, and parsley in cheesecloth. Tie it with cotton string, leaving a length that can be tied to the handle of the pot (this will facilitate easy removal).

Add the bouquet garni and salt and pepper and place the pot, uncovered, in the oven for 45 minutes. Remove from the oven and taste for seasoning.

Traditionally, the soup is ladled into an individual crock or ramekin, topped with a piece of toasted bread and a layer of Gruyère cheese, and placed under a broiler briefly to melt the cheese and give it a light toast.

INDONESIAN PEANUT-CELERY SOUP
BAYONA
SUSAN SPICER, CHEF/OWNER

New Orleans ★

Further tribute to Chef Spicer's international inspirations, this wonderful soup combines the earthiness of peanut butter with Asian spice. Ketjap manis is Indonesian soy sauce, which is sweeter than traditional soy sauce and a thicker, almost syrup-like consistency. Sambal oelek is ground red chile paste. Look for both products in Asian markets or order online.

Heat the oil in a 2-quart pot over medium heat and add the onion, celery, and garlic. Cook, stirring, for about 5 minutes, until the vegetables have softened. Reduce heat to low, cover pot, and let steam for about 10 minutes, stirring once.

Remove cover and add the chicken stock, then whisk in the peanut butter a little at a time. Bring to a boil, whisking, and add the ketjap manis and sambal oelek. Add a little more stock or water if soup is too thick. Simmer about 10 minutes, then remove from heat and let cool.

Working in batches if necessary, purée the soup in a blender and return to the pot. Heat soup to the desired temperature, adjust seasonings (adding more chile paste, if desired), and consistency (adding more stock or water if needed). Garnish with roasted peanuts and serve.

SERVES 6 TO 8

2 tablespoons cooking oil, such as peanut or canola

1 medium onion, chopped

1 bunch celery, trimmed and chopped

2 cloves garlic, minced

4 to 5 cups chicken stock (or vegetable stock or water)

1 cup creamy peanut butter

¼ cup ketjap manis

1 teaspoon sambal oelek (or other red chile paste)

Salt, to taste

¼ cup chopped dry-roasted peanuts, for garnish

New Orleans

SERVES 8 TO 10

Vegetable oil

1 pound coarse chopped turtle meat

1 pound course ground meat (beef or veal)

1 teaspoon salt

1 teaspoon freshly ground black pepper

1 teaspoon garlic powder

1 large onion, chopped

1 bell pepper, chopped (seeds removed)

½ bunch celery chopped

2 cups crushed tomatoes

6 cups chicken stock

½ pound unsalted butter

1 cup all-purpose flour

1 cup fresh spinach, finely chopped

2 hard-boiled eggs, coarsely chopped

¼ cup dry sherry (optional), plus more for serving

TURTLE SOUP
THE LE MOYNE DE BIENVILLE CLUB
COREY NOLAN, CHEF

In 1718, New Orleans was established by the French-Canadian explorer Jen Baptiste Le Moyne Sieur de Bienville. The Le Moyne de Bienville Club, one of the city's private social clubs, was founded in 1964. Turtle soup—as traditional in New Orleans as gumbo—is by far the most popular item on the Club's menu, according to General Manager Kenneth L. Verlander, Jr. Noting that people will order turtle soup at every restaurant they visit for comparison, he proudly states that many have called theirs the best in the city. Look for turtle meat in Asian markets; or order it online.

Cover the bottom of a large stock pot with vegetable oil and allow to get hot. Add the turtle meat and ground meat with salt, pepper and garlic powder and cook until the liquid has cooked away and the meat begins to brown. Stir frequently to get the "goodness" from the caramelizing meat. Add the chopped onion, bell pepper, and celery and cook until they are lightly browned. Add the tomatoes, lower the heat and cook slowly until the mixture is a rich red-brown color. Add the stock, turn up the heat and bring to a boil. Once it begins to boil, lower the heat and simmer for 1 hour.

While the stock is simmering, make a roux. In a skillet, melt the butter and slowly add the flour until absorbed. Cook, stirring constantly, until it is a light peanut-butter color. Slowly whisk the roux into the simmering stock a little at a time.

After the soup has simmered for 1 hour, add the chopped spinach, eggs, and sherry, if using. Turn the heat off, but leave the soup on the stove for 30 minutes more, stirring occasionally. Taste and adjust seasoning accordingly.

Serve with dry sherry on the side.

BOUILLABAISSE
LA TRUFFE SAUVAGE
MOHAMED CHETTOUH, CHEF

A fisherman's stew traditionally made with the unsold fish from their catch. Nowadays, it is prepared with premium seafood in most restaurants, although using what is on hand works very well. The key is timing the addition of the seafood so everything is cooked appropriately when it's time to serve. With preparation, this dish can be cooked and served in a brief period of time.

Serve this with homemade croutons of garlic bread: slice a baguette and drizzle with olive oil before toasting in a hot oven. Rub lightly with cut fresh garlic once cooled. A dollop of aioli (a Provençal garlic mayonnaise) is great with this too!

Place the potatoes in a saucepan and cover with cold water. Add the saffron and some salt; bring to a boil and simmer until done. Drain, and set aside.

Using a rondeau (a large pot with low sides), heat until moderately hot. Season the fish and seafood with salt and pepper. Lightly dust one side of the fish in flour. Pour a generous amount of olive oil in the pan and sear the floured side of the fish, shrimp, and other seafood until it has a nice brown color (this step is to build overall flavor, not to cook the fish). Remove and set aside.

Pour off the excess oil and return the pan to heat. Add more olive oil and lightly brown the garlic and shallots. Add the fennel, tomato sauce, white wine, potatoes, and a generous amount of stock. Season with salt and pepper. Bring to a boil, then reduce heat to a strong simmer.

Add seafood according to the time it needs to be cooked. Most of the seared seafood can be added at the same time, unless it happens to be thick cut of fish.

When the fish is cooked, turn off heat; add more olive oil (about 2 ounces) and parsley. Adjust the seasoning to taste and serve with croutons.

Lake Charles

SERVES 4

6 medium-sized red potatoes, peeled

Pinch of saffron

1 teaspoon salt

1½ to 2 pounds mix of Louisiana or Gulf fish, shellfish, and crustaceans

Sea salt and freshly ground black pepper

¼ cup flour, for dusting

1 cup or more olive oil

4 cloves garlic, minced

1 shallot or small onion, diced small

1 piece fennel, diced medium

2 cups tomato sauce (prepared with fresh tomatoes)

1 cup white wine

3 to 4 cups fish stock, or light chicken stock

¼ bunch parsley, minced

Baton Rouge
★

2 teaspoons liquid crab boil

3 medium potatoes, peeled

3 to 4 slices bacon

4 cups chopped yellow onions

1½ cups chopped green bell peppers

1 tablespoon salt

½ teaspoon freshly ground black pepper

1 teaspoon cayenne pepper

1 teaspoon ground thyme

1 pound Louisiana crawfish tails

1½ pounds fresh, peeled tiny (90/110) Louisiana shrimp

4 cups low-fat milk

SEAFOOD CHOWDER
MIKE ANDERSON'S SEAFOOD
MIKE ANDERSON, OWNER

In the more than 35 years since former LSU All-American football player first opened Mike Anderson's College Town Seafood & Oyster Bar, the restaurant has become a southern Louisiana institution.

During refrigeration, the chowder may thicken. If so, add a small amount of milk when reheating and stir until desired consistency. Thyme is the ingredient that gives this chowder its unique taste.

In a medium pot, combine crab boil and 4 cups of water. Bring to a boil. Add potatoes. Cook over high heat until potatoes are tender. Drain and set aside.

Fry the bacon until well done. Set the bacon aside and pour the bacon fat into a medium-sized pot with lid. Add the onions and pepper and sauté. Cover and simmer 15 to 20 minutes over low heat. Quarter the cooked potatoes and add them to the pot, along with the salt, black pepper, cayenne, and thyme. Stir. Add the crawfish, shrimp, and reserved bacon. Stir. Cook over medium heat until shrimp are done (3 to 5 minutes, or until they turn pink). Add the milk and continue to simmer until creamy.

AUDREY MARSH, *SPLASH OF FLAVOR, OIL AND ACRYLIC*

New Orleans ★

SHRIMP BISQUE
BRIGTSEN'S RESTAURANT
FRANK BRIGTSEN, EXECUTIVE CHEF/OWNER

James Beard Award–winning Chef Brigtsen, a NOLA native, trained under no less a master than Chef Paul Prudhomme, rising to Executive Chef at K-Paul's Louisiana Kitchen before opening his own restaurant in 1986. Since then, he has garnered local and national praise for his inventive take on Creole/Acadian cooking. When inducted into the LRA Hall of Fame in 2012, Chef Brigtsen said: "When I put this chef coat on, I'm putting on 200 years of Louisiana history and it's truly an honor."

SERVES 12

4 pounds fresh head-on Louisiana shrimp (see Note)

1¼ cups vegetable oil

1½ cups all-purpose flour

2 tablespoons unsalted butter

4 cups diced yellow onions

3 cups diced celery

2 cups diced green bell peppers

2 bay leaves

2 tablespoons minced fresh garlic

7 teaspoons salt

¼ teaspoon white pepper

½ teaspoon freshly ground black pepper

½ teaspoon cayenne pepper

½ teaspoon dried whole-leaf thyme

2 teaspoons dried whole-leaf sweet basil

Make the shrimp stock. Peel and clean the shrimp. Set the peeled shrimp aside (you should have 4 cups) and add the shrimp heads and shells to a large pot, with 13 cups of cold water. Bring to a boil. Reduce heat to low and simmer for 15 minutes. Strain and set the shrimp stock aside.

Make a dark brown roux. Heat the vegetable oil in a cast-iron skillet over medium-high heat until it reaches frying temperature (375°F). Gradually add the flour, whisking constantly. Cook, whisking constantly, until the roux begins to thicken and brown. Reduce heat to low and cook, stirring constantly, until the roux is dark brown (chocolate-colored). Remove from heat and set aside.

In a separate pot, heat the butter over high heat. Add the onions, celery, bell peppers, and bay leaves. Cook, stirring occasionally, until the onions turn soft and clear. Add the garlic, salt, white pepper, black pepper, cayenne, thyme, and basil. Cook, stirring constantly, for 1 to 2 minutes. Add the peeled shrimp and cook, stirring occasionally, for 2 to 3 minutes. Add 12 cups of shrimp stock to the mixture and bring to a boil.

Pour off any excess oil that may have risen to the top of the roux and discard. Slowly and carefully add the roux to the boiling mixture, whisking constantly. Reduce heat to low and simmer, stirring occasionally, for 10 minutes. Skim off any excess oil that rises to the top of the pot and discard.

Remove the 2 bay leaves and discard. Use an immersion blender to puree the bisque (or carefully transfer the mixture to a blender and puree in batches). To serve, ladle 1½ cups of bisque into each large soup bowl. Serve immediately.

Note: This is a Cajun shrimp bisque, which utilizes a dark brown roux for body and flavor. The shrimp stock is also a vital part of the recipe. Peel your shrimp and save the heads and/or shells to make shrimp stock. In general, 1 pound of fresh, head-on shrimp will yield about 1 cup of peeled shrimp. Therefore, this recipe requires about 4 pounds of fresh, head-on shrimp. The shrimp will be pureed, so small or medium shrimp are fine.

MEGAN PIERCE, *RAGIN' CAJUN CRAWFISH*, COLORED PENCIL

Shreveport

40 Louisiana crawfish tails

1 tablespoon butter

1 medium onion, chopped

1 cup chopped mustard greens

1 cup uncooked white rice

4 cups chicken or vegetable stock

3 ounces pecans, roasted and coarsely chopped

¼ teaspoon cayenne pepper, or to taste

Salt and freshly ground black pepper, to taste

½ cup grated Parmesan cheese, for serving

CRAWFISH AND PECAN SOUP
RISTORANTE GIUSEPPE
GIUSEPPE BRUCIA, CHEF/OWNER

A native of Sicily, Chef Brucia apprenticed in Milan, and established his reputation in restaurants across Italy, Germany, and Switzerland before arriving on American shores.

He has been a part of the Shreveport community for more than 30 years, and has had four different restaurants during that time. This recipe was created for a celebration of Creole cuisine at his first restaurant, Firenze's, and is still served during special events.

Bring a large pot of water to a boil and add the crawfish. Cook for 2 minutes, remove the crawfish from the pot, and set aside.

In a saucepan over medium heat, melt the butter and sauté the onion until it begins to sweat. Stir in the mustard greens and rice. Add the stock and bring to a boil. Reduce heat to medium and cook until the rice is tender, 15 to 20 minutes.

Stir in the pecans and add the cayenne and salt and pepper to taste. Add the crawfish meat and stir to combine. Serve in bowls and top with Parmesan cheese.

CREAM OF BRIE CHEESE AND LUMP CRABMEAT SOUP
MANSURS ON THE BOULEVARD
TIM KRINGLIE, CORPORATE CHEF

This velvety soup, typical of the restaurant's elegant Creole cuisine, has been on the Mansurs's menu since it opened in 1989, and was awarded a Gold medal by the American Culinary Foundation Baton Rouge Chapter.

Heat 3 tablespoons of the butter in a 5-quart pot and sauté the onion, bell pepper, and celery until tender. In another small saucepan, start a roux by melting the remaining ½ cup butter; whisk in the flour until smooth and blended. Let the roux cook, stirring often, until "blond" (golden brown and toasty), about 20 minutes.

Add the crab base, half-and-half, white pepper, Tabasco, vermouth, lemon juice, Creole seasoning, and garlic to the pot. Bring to a slow boil and thicken with 2 ounces of the hot blond roux. Stir continuously until smooth and silky. Add the Brie and the crabmeat when ready to serve. (Do not bring to a boil after the cheese has been added.)

Note: Crab base is concentrated crab stock; look for it in paste, powder, or cube form in Asian markets, at specialty stores, or online.

Baton Rouge
★

SERVES 8

½ cup plus 3 tablespoons unsalted butter, divided

1 medium onion, finely diced

1 medium bell pepper, finely diced

2 ribs celery, finely diced

½ cup all-purpose flour

2 tablespoons crab base (see Note)

6 cups half-and-half

¼ teaspoon white pepper

¼ teaspoon Tabasco sauce

1 tablespoon dry vermouth

⅛ teaspoon lemon juice

1 teaspoon Creole seasoning

1 teaspoon chopped garlic

6 ounces Brie, outer rind removed

8 ounces fresh Louisiana crabmeat (do not use frozen)

Covington ★

2 sticks butter

1 onion, diced

4 ribs celery, diced

2 green bell peppers, diced

Salt and freshly ground pepper, to taste

4 cloves garlic, minced

2 to 3 cups all-purpose flour (more yields a thicker soup)

2 bay leaves

2 teaspoons dried thyme leaf

4 tablespoons Crystal hot sauce

2 cups white wine

2 cups heavy cream

3 quarts crab or seafood stock

3 pounds fresh chanterelle mushrooms (other mushrooms may be substituted)

1 pound jumbo lump Louisiana crabmeat, picked

CREAM OF LOUISIANA BLUE CRAB SOUP
LOLA
KEITH AND NEALY FRENTZ, CHEFS/OWNERS

Keith and Nealy Frentz met when both held sous chef positions at New Orleans's famous Brennan's Restaurant. Evacuating after Katrina to Keith's hometown of Covington, opening LOLA in 2006. The restaurant is housed in the city's historic train depot and serves the couple's contemporary take on classic Louisiana dishes.

Melt the butter in a large pot over medium heat. Add the onion, celery, bell peppers, salt, and pepper and sauté until the vegetables are soft, about 10 minutes. Add the garlic.

Stir in flour to make a roux (use 2 cups for a thinner soup, up to 3 if you prefer it thicker). Whisk until the flour is fully incorporated. Cook an additional 3 to 4 minutes, stirring often. Add the bay leaves, thyme, hot sauce, wine, cream, and stock. Cook over medium-low heat until mixture starts to thicken, about 20 minutes.

Add the mushrooms and cook until they become tender. Adjust seasoning. Turn off the fire and gently stir in the crabmeat. Let sit until crab is heated through; serve warm.

CORN AND CRAB BISQUE
SLAP YA MAMA
WALKER & SONS, OWNERS

Ville Platte

Take advantage of fresh corn in season when making this classic Cajun soup. The dish gets an extra kick from the addition of the Walker family's Slap Ya Mama Cajun Seasoning.

Heat the butter in a large pot over medium heat. Add the onions and cook until soft and translucent. Pour in the chicken broth, and bring to a boil. Stir in the garlic, bay leaves and Slap Ya Mama Cajun Seasoning to taste. Stir the corn into boiling broth. Reduce heat to medium low and simmer about 10 minutes.

Remove 1 cup of the soup and set aside to cool slightly. Pour into a food processor, add the half-and-half, and puree for 30 to 45 seconds. Set aside.

In a small bowl, stir together the flour and milk until smooth. Slowly stir the slurry into the simmering soup. Stirring constantly, simmer for 1 to 2 minutes, then stir in the pureed mixture.

Reduce heat to low, stir in crabmeat, and cook until the crabmeat is warmed through, about 5 minutes.

MAKES 8 SERVINGS

4 tablespoons butter

¾ cup chopped onion

3 (14-ounce) cans chicken broth

3 cloves garlic

2 bay leaves

Slap Ya Mama Cajun Seasoning (White Pepper Blend), to taste

2½ cups fresh corn kernels (4 ears corn)

½ cup half-and-half

3 tablespoons all-purpose flour

½ cup milk

16 ounces fresh jumbo lump Louisiana crabmeat

New Orleans ★

FOR THE SALAD:

4 cups mixed salad greens

4 tablespoons crumbled crisp bacon

4 tablespoons freshly grated Parmesan cheese

1 cup croutons

FOR THE COMMANDER'S DRESSING:

(MAKES 2 CUPS)

1½ cups salad oil

1 egg, at room temperature

⅓ teaspoon salt

½ teaspoon freshly cracked peppercorns

¼ cup white vinegar

3 tablespoons minced onions

2 hard-cooked eggs, halved, for garnish

COMMANDER'S SALAD
COMMANDER'S PALACE
TORY McPHAIL, EXECUTIVE CHEF

First opened in 1880, this Garden District landmark has been in the hands of the esteemed Brennan family since 1974. Tory McPhail is the latest in a line of chefs that include Paul Prudhomme and Emeril Lagasse; McPhail won the James Beard Award for Best Chef: South in 2013. Here is the restaurant's most popular side salad, a colorful combination that uses the freshest seasonal salad greens, including leaf lettuce, field lettuce, Bibb, romaine, oak leaf, endive, and watercress.

Make the salad. Wash and dry the greens and tear into bite-size pieces. In a salad bowl, combine the greens, bacon, Parmesan, and croutons.

Make the dressing. Put ½ cup of the oil and the egg, salt, pepper, vinegar, and onion in a blender. Cover and blend on low speed. Remove cover and gradually blend in the remaining oil.

To serve, pour 8 tablespoons dressing over the salad and toss. Divide onto individual salad plates or into bowls, and garnish each serving with hard-cooked egg half.

SPRING MIX SALAD WITH CHAMPAGNE VINAIGRETTE
LAKESHORE HIGH SCHOOL
JUDY ARCHERY, PROSTART INSTRUCTOR

Mandeville ★

Donated by a mentor chef from La Provence, John Besh's French cuisine restaurant in Lacombe, Louisiana, this salad gained the school Third Place in the Louisiana Seafood ProStart Culinary Competition. Sweet pecans combine with savory goat cheese and a tangy vinaigrette for a wonderful blend of flavors.

Make the candied pecans. Preheat the oven to 350°F. Lightly oil a baking sheet and line it with parchment paper. Put a medium-sized pan over medium heat. Add the sugar and let it melt. Meanwhile, in another bowl, whisk the egg white until frothy. Add in your pecans and stir so that all the nuts are evenly coated. Then add the pecans to the melted sugar and stir so that all the nuts are evenly coated. Place the pecans evenly and in a single layer across the prepared baking sheet. Bake for 11 minutes (until golden and covered in a smooth glaze of caramel). Set aside to cool.

Make the vinaigrette. In a small bowl, whisk together the Champagne, Champagne vinegar, sugar, oil, salt, and pepper.

To serve the salad, toss the mixed greens in a large bowl with the Champagne vinaigrette. Divide the dressed greens onto two salad plates and sprinkle each with the goat cheese and candied pecans.

SERVES 2

FOR THE CANDIED PECANS:

½ cup sugar

1 egg white

1 cup pecans

FOR THE CHAMPAGNE VINAIGRETTE:

1 tablespoon Champagne

¼ cup Champagne vinegar

Pinch of sugar

1 cup canola oil

Pinch of salt and freshly ground black pepper

FOR THE SALAD:

2 cups spring mix

1 cup arugula

2 ounces goat cheese, crumbled

Lafayette

SERVES 2

FOR THE SESAME-SOY DRESSING:

½ cup rice wine vinegar

½ cup soy sauce

2 tablespoons sesame oil

½ cup sugar

2 tablespoons sesame seeds

FOR THE SALAD:

4 cups mixed greens

1 avocado, sliced

1 Roma tomato, sliced

2 carrots, julienned

1 (6-ounce) chicken breast, grilled and cut into strips, or

8 jumbo (21/25) Louisiana shrimp, grilled, or

1 (6-ounce) tuna steak, cooked to desired temperature and sliced

TSUNAMI SALAD WITH SESAME-SOY DRESSING
TSUNAMI
LEAH SIMON, MICHELE EZELL, OWNERS

Tsunami serves sushi and other Asian fare—and serves as a fixture of Lafayette's downtown social scene. At the restaurant, this signature salad is served with a choice of grilled chicken or shrimp, or seared tuna.

Make the sesame-soy dressing. Add the rice wine vinegar, soy sauce, and sesame oil to a mixing bowl and whisk until well combined. Add the sugar and sesame seeds, and continue to whisk until the sugar is dissolved. Set aside

Make the salad. Add the greens to a large bowl and mix with dressing. Divide the dressed greens onto 2 plates. Divide the avocado and tomato slices onto the greens, and sprinkle the carrots over. Distribute the chicken, shrimp, or tuna evenly among the plates and serve.

BELLE RIVER CRAWFISH SALAD
ARNAUD'S RESTAURANT
TOMMY DIGIOVANNI, CHEF DE CUISINE

New Orleans

This is a seasonal dish that is offered by the restaurant during crawfish season—from January to June, when Louisiana harvests more than 110 million pounds of these little lobsters. Often the daily special, the chef suggests that this salad tastes best on top of a fried green tomato. Note that this salad is best prepared one day before serving.

In a small mixing bowl combine the onions, celery, relish, parsley, mayonnaise, ketchup, Worcestershire sauce, lemon juice, Tabasco, salt, and pepper.

Add the crawfish and gently fold the sauce over the tails, just until they are lightly coated. Wrap tightly and refrigerate for 24 hours before serving. Serve alone, with assorted greens or seasonal vegetables, or on top of a fried green tomato.

SERVES 6

¾ cup small diced red onion

¾ cup small diced green onion

¾ cup small diced celery

¼ cup pickle relish

¾ cup chopped parsley

1½ cups mayonnaise

¾ cup ketchup

1 tablespoon Worcester-shire sauce

Juice of 2 lemons (about ⅓ cup)

1 tablespoon Tabasco sauce

Salt and pepper, to taste

6 cups Louisiana crawfish tails

SERVES 6

FOR THE CRABMEAT:

24 ounces fresh mozzarella

24 Creole tomatoes

Kosher salt, to taste

Freshly ground black pepper, to taste

3 teaspoons finely chopped basil

6 (1-ounce) portions of mixed greens

3 ounces balsamic vinegar

1½ ounces extra virgin olive oil

¾ ounce yellow onion, finely chopped

1 pound Louisiana crabmeat

FOR THE RAVIGOTE SAUCE:

¼ cup Champagne vinegar

½ teaspoon salt

Pinch of freshly ground black pepper

1 tablespoon minced shallot

1 tablespoon minced capers

1 teaspoon Dijon mustard

1 cup vegetable oil

CREOLE CRABMEAT CAPRÈSE
RALPH BRENNAN'S CAFÉ NOMA
CHRIS MONTERO, EXECUTIVE CHEF

The classic French sauce ravigote is a highly seasoned vinaigrette. Ravigote means reinvigorated, and the sauce is customarily served with mild-flavored foods. Here, it gives a Creole twist to the classic Italian Caprèse salad with added crabmeat—a perfect dish to enjoy at this café within the New Orleans Museum of Art. Creole tomatoes are large, round vine-ripened tomatoes that begin to appear in southern Louisiana gardens and markets in early June.

Slice the mozzarella into 1-ounce rounds; cut the tomatoes in ¼-inch slices. Alternately layer the tomatoes and fresh mozzarella rounds on a plate. Season with salt and pepper and sprinkle with basil.

Whisk together the balsamic vinegar and olive oil. In a mixing bowl, toss mixed greens with half of the balsamic vinaigrette, salt and pepper. Place the greens on the plate next to the tomatoes and mozzarella.

Sprinkle the onions on top of the greens and drizzle the remainder of the dressing on the tomatoes.

To finish, gently fold the crabmeat and 2 tablespoons of the ravigote sauce in a bowl. Top the salad with 3 ounces of the crabmeat-ravigote mixture.

RAVIGOTE SAUCE
Whisk together the vinegar, salt, pepper, shallots, capers and mustard—keep whisking the mixture until the salt dissolves.

Add the oil in a slow steady stream, whisking constantly. Don't rush this; add the oil slowly.

The dressing will keep, refrigerated in a covered container, for 1 week. Pour over mixed greens.

ALEXA HOLLAND, *A PERFECT CRAWFISH,* OIL AND ACRYLIC (EIGHTH PLACE SENIOR)

New Orleans ★

SERVES 4

FOR THE RÉMOULADE SAUCE:

½ yellow onion, chopped

¼ cup Dijon mustard

½ cup Creole mustard (see Note)

½ cup ketchup

¼ cup prepared horseradish

2 ribs celery, finely chopped

3 sprigs parsley, finely chopped

2 eggs

½ tablespoon finely chopped garlic

1 tablespoon Crystal hot sauce

¼ bunch green onion, chopped

¼ lemon (rind and pulp), de-seeded

¾ cup vegetable oil

Salt, to taste

TOMATO BLEU CHEESE NAPOLEON
DICKIE BRENNAN'S STEAKHOUSE
ALFRED SINGLETON, EXECUTIVE CHEF

A signature dish since its opening in 1998, the Tomato Bleu Cheese Napoleon is a popular way to start a meal at Dickie Brennan's Steakhouse. Located in the heart of the French Quarter, the restaurant serves prime steaks with a New Orleans touch. What else would one expect from this scion of NOLA's first family of food?

Make the rémoulade sauce. Place the yellow onion, Dijon and Creole mustards, ketchup, horseradish, celery, parsley, eggs, garlic, hot sauce, green onion, and lemon in a food processor and process until smooth. Slowly add the oil until emulsified. Adjust seasoning to taste and set aside.

Make the Napoleon. Toss the julienned lettuce in the cane vinegar; add salt and pepper to taste. Divide onto four salad plates and place one slice of tomato on top; add salt and pepper to taste. Crumble 2 ounces of bleu cheese on top and layer with another slice of tomato. Pour 6 tablespoons of rémoulade sauce over the tomato and top with another 2 ounces of bleu cheese. Garnish with shaved red onions and a garlic crostini.

Note: Creole mustard is a piquant grainy mustard. Look for it on the grocery shelves of national retailers or order online.

FOR THE TOMATO NAPOLEON:

1 head green leaf lettuce, julienned

¼ cup cane vinegar (see Note, page 25)

Salt and freshly ground black pepper, to taste

2 tomatoes, sliced thick

16 ounces bleu cheese

1½ cups rémoulade sauce

1 red onion, thinly sliced

Garlic crostini, for serving

MASON WATSON, *DINNER BY THE DOCK,* OIL AND ACRYLIC

Lutcher

FOR THE HOMEMADE DRESSING:

1 cup vegetable oil

¾ cup sugar

2 cloves garlic, finely chopped

½ teaspoon salt

½ teaspoon paprika

¼ teaspoon white pepper

FOR THE SALAD:

1 (5-ounce) bag Spring Mix lettuce

1 (10-ounce) bag hearts of Romaine lettuce

1 cup sliced strawberries

1 (8-ounce) bag finely shredded Monterey Jack cheese

1 cup walnut pieces

STRAWBERRY AND WALNUT SALAD WITH HOMEMADE DRESSING

ST. JAMES CAREER AND TECHNOLOGY CENTER
ASHLEY LOUQUE, PROSTART STUDENT

This recipe has been in Ashley's family for years and it would not be a family occasion without it. Created by her late Aunt Mim, the salad is a fond reminder of her. Ashley took Second Place in her school's Food Fest competition with this recipe.

Make the dressing. Put the oil, sugar, garlic, salt, paprika, and pepper in a jar with a tight lid and shake hard until the sugar dissolves, or put all the ingredients in a blender and run until sugar is dissolved.

Make the salad. Place the lettuces and strawberries in a large bowl; pour the dressing over and toss until well mixed. Sprinkle the cheese and walnut pieces across the top; toss once more just before serving.

WATERMELON, CUCUMBER, AND FETA SALAD

BAYONA
SUSAN SPICER, CHEF/OWNER

Elected to the James Beard Foundation's Who's Who of Food & Beverage in America, Susan Spicer co-owns the four-star Bayona with business partner Regina Keever. The restaurant is housed in a 200-year-old French Quarter cottage with an outdoor courtyard.

Make the dressing. Whisk together the lemon and lime juices with the honey in a small bowl, then add the olive oil, mint, salt, and cayenne and whisk until the salt is dissolved.

Make the salad. Toss the watermelon, cucumber, arugula, onion, and dressing together in a large salad bowl. Divide the salad evenly among four plates. Top the salads with equal portions of the crumbled feta cheese.

New Orleans
★

SERVES 4

FOR THE CITRUS DRESSING:

1 tablespoon fresh lemon juice

2 tablespoons fresh lime juice

2 teaspoons honey

⅓ cup olive oil

1 tablespoon chopped fresh mint

Salt, to taste

Pinch of cayenne pepper

FOR THE SALAD

2 cups ripe red or yellow watermelon (or a combination of both), seeded and diced

2 cups cucumber, seeded and diced

1 bunch arugula or 2 cups spinach, washed and dried

1 small red onion, cut in half and thinly sliced

¼ cup feta cheese, crumbled

SERVES 4

¼ medium yellow water-melon

¼ medium red water-melon

1 cup cane vinegar (see Note, page 25)

3 tablespoons sugar, divided

Juice of 2 lemons (about ⅓ cup)

8 sprigs mint, picked, divided

¼ cup Buffalo Trace Whiskey

½ cup vegetable oil

Pinch of kosher salt

Pinch of freshly ground black pepper

1 head Bibb lettuce, rinsed

WATERMELON SALAD WITH BUFFALO TRACE SMASH VINAIGRETTE
COMMANDER'S PALACE
TORY MCPHAIL, EXECUTIVE CHEF

Chef McPhail bases his Creole-American menu on the availability of the freshest local ingredients. This light summer salad is high-lighted by quick-pickled watermelon rind and a dressing that incorporates Buffalo Trace Whiskey. Although imported from Kentucky, the distillery is owned by the Sazerac Company, a New Orleans–based producer/importer.

Remove and discard the rind from the yellow watermelon. Cut the green skin from the red watermelon and, using a veg-etable peeler, shave enough 2-inch strips from the white rind to measure ½ cup. Place the peelings in a stainless steel bowl. Remove and discard the rest of the rind from the watermelon. Bring the cane vinegar and 2 tablespoons of the sugar to boil in a medium saucepot. Pour over the rind slices, and let stand for 45 minutes.

In another stainless steel bowl, muddle half the mint with the remaining sugar and the lemon juice. Stir in the whiskey and oil, season with the salt and pepper.

Cut both watermelons into 2-inch by ½-inch thick squares, removing as many seeds as possible. Tear the lettuce into large pieces and toss with watermelon squares and vinaigrette. Arrange on four salad plates, and garnish with the pickled rind and remaining mint.

REBECCA MAPLES, *MARKS OF LOUISIANA,* OIL AND ACRYLIC
(FOURTH PLACE SENIOR)

CHAPTER THREE

POULTRY AND MEAT

New Orleans ★

SERVES 4

1 fryer chicken, cut into 8 pieces

Salt and freshly ground pepper

1 gallon vegetable oil

2 baking potatoes

¼ cup clarified butter

1 pound large button mushrooms, cleaned and sliced

3 tablespoons minced garlic

Salt and freshly ground white pepper to taste

1 (15-ounce) can petit pois peas, drained

Chopped curly parsley, for garnish

CHICKEN CLEMENCEAU
GALATOIRE'S
MICHAEL SICHEL, EXECUTIVE CHEF

French statesman Georges Clemenceau (1841–1929) is credited with bringing France from the brink of defeat to victory in World War I. In part he did so by convincing the Allies to unify their efforts through the leadership of a supreme commander, previously unheard of among nations of the day. Equally unheard of was the amalgamation of chicken, fried potatoes, garlic, mushrooms and canned peas into a single dish, as was achieved at Galatoire's in the 1920s to delicious effect. The dish is named for Monsieur Clemenceau. This is one of the specialties of the house at this grande dame of New Orleans restaurants, which was founded in 1905.

Preheat the oven to 400°F. Rinse the chicken pieces and dry thoroughly. Season the chicken generously with salt and pepper and bake on a rimmed baking sheet for approximately 30 minutes, until golden brown, turning the pieces after 15 minutes.

While the chicken is baking, heat the oil to 350°F in a large heavy-bottomed pot. Peel the potatoes and dice them into ¾-inch cubes. When the oil is hot, add the potatoes, about 1 cup at a time. The moisture content in the potatoes will make the oil boil up, so use a long handled spoon when adding. Fry the potatoes in batches, 7 to 9 minutes each batch, until golden brown, moving the cubes around with the spoon to ensure that all sides brown evenly. Remove the potatoes from the oil with a slotted spoon and drain on paper towels.

Heat the butter in a large sauté pan over high heat, then add the mushrooms. Cook the mushrooms for about 5 minutes, until tender. Add the garlic and the fried potatoes. Season with salt and white pepper and sauté briefly to heat through. Add the chicken pieces and sauté for 3 to 5 minutes, until the flavors marry. Gently fold in the petit pois and cook until just heated through.

Divide the chicken Clemenceau among four dinner plates using a slotted spoon to drain any excess butter. Finish the dish by sprinkling each portion with chopped parsley. Serve immediately.

SARAH BRAUNS, *GROSS ÉCREVISSE*, MIXED MEDIA

CHICKEN AND DUMPLINGS
THE AMERICAN SECTOR
JOHN BESH, OWNER/JEFF MATTIA, CHEF

New Orleans

★

SERVES 4

2 tablespoons salt

1 tablespoon sugar

6 boneless, skinless chicken thighs, cut in bite-sized pieces

1 cup ricotta cheese

3 egg yolks

¼ teaspoon salt

Pinch of nutmeg

⅓ cup flour

1 tablespoon olive oil

3 shallots, minced

2 cloves garlic, minced

1 teaspoon minced ginger

1 teaspoon crushed red pepper flakes

1 gallon chicken stock

1 cup chanterelle mushrooms, chopped

1 sprig thyme

1 sprig sage, chopped

½ cup sweet peas

1 tomato, peeled, seeded, and diced

2 tablespoons butter

Salt and pepper

4 sprigs chervil, for garnish

Chef Mattia serves an eclectic menu of American comfort food, traditional Louisiana dishes, and innovative contemporary cuisine at this restaurant within the National WWII Museum. In addition to the main restaurant, there is the Soda Shop, serving sundaes, sandwiches, and other fun fare inspired by WWII-era cuiine. This updated version of the classic features dumplings made with ricotta cheese for a lighter texture.

In a mixing bowl combine the salt and sugar in 1 quart of cold water. Stir to dissolve. Add the chicken and refrigerate for 1 hour. While the chicken is brining, combine the ricotta with the egg yolks, salt, and nutmeg. Slowly stir in just enough flour to form a dough with the cheese. Blanch the dumplings in lightly salted water and then shock them in cold water to stop the cooking. Remove them from the cold water and reserve in refrigerator.

Remove chicken from brine and pat dry with paper towels. Sear in a deep sauté pan with the olive oil over high heat. Add the shallots, garlic, ginger, and pepper flakes to the pan. Lower the heat to medium and cook 5 minutes before adding chicken stock. Slowly simmer until the liquid reduces by nearly half. Add the mushrooms, thyme, sage, peas, and tomato. Add the butter and season to taste with salt and pepper before adding the dumplings to the pan. Serve in bowls, garnished with chervil.

CHICKEN, PORK, AND SAUSAGE JAMBALAYA

NICHOLAS CATERING

EMERY T. NICHOLAS, JR., CHEF/OWNER

Thibodaux ★

Nicholas Catering has been serving the families and businesses of South Louisiana for years. Of his version of this classic Louisiana dish, Chef Nicholas says, "This recipe is a simple Cajun dish that my mom taught me and her mom taught her, and so on down the line. For them, it was a way to easily feed a big family without a lot of expense—with the added bonus of being all in one pot for easy clean up! What my mom also liked about doing a simple jambalaya was that you didn't have to always use chicken, pork, or sausage. Really you were able to use whatever meat you had in the house. Although I think the best mix is chicken, pork, and sausage, I've been known to throw in some duck, deer, or even a stray squirrel or two. I am a Cajun Boy at heart!"

In a large pot, brown the pork over high heat (add a little water to avoid sticking). Cook for about 25 minutes over medium heat then add the onions, bell pepper, and garlic. Cook for about 10 minutes more; the mixture should be boiling.

Once it comes to a boil, add the sausage, chicken, rice, green onions, Kitchen Bouquet, water, and Creole seasoning. Stir it well, cover, and reduce the heat to low. After 15 minutes, stir, and re-cover. Check again in in 30 minutes; it should be done .

SERVES 12 TO 16

2 pounds pork loin, cubed

1 cup chopped onions

2 green bell peppers, seeded and chopped

1 tablespoon minced garlic

2 pounds sausage, thickly sliced

1 pound boneless, skinless chicken thighs, cubed

2 pounds parboiled rice

1 bunch green onions, sliced

2 tablespoons Kitchen Bouquet

8 tablespoons Tony Chachere's Creole Seasoning (or whatever brand you prefer)

1 bunch parsley, minced

Lafayette ★

SERVES 6

FOR THE POTATOES:

10 sweet potatoes, peeled and quartered

1 cup heavy cream, warmed

½ cup honey

Salt and freshly ground black pepper, to taste

FOR THE DUCK:

6 boneless duck breasts, skin on

Salt and freshly ground black pepper, to taste

4 bottles Cane Sugar Root Beer

1 quart fig syrup

FOR THE GREEN BEANS:

2 tablespoons vegetable oil

1 pound haricot verts (trimmed, blanched and shocked in ice water to preserve color)

¼ cup honey

1 tablespoon Creole seasoning

¼ cup chopped pecans

CAST-IRON DUCK BREAST WITH FIG AND ROOT BEER GLAZE
BLUE DOG CAFÉ
STEVE SANTILLO/ANDRE RODRIGUE, OWNERS

Those who love great food—and great art—flock to this hot spot in the heart of Cajun country. The café walls display a vast collection of George Rodrigue's Blue Dog paintings, while the tables are graced with sophisticated takes on traditional Bayou cuisine. Its popular Sunday brunch features live music in styles ranging from Celtic to Swamp Pop to Zydeco. This delicious duck is served with sweet potatoes and greenbeans.

Make the potatoes. Boil the sweet potatoes until tender, strain and return them to the pan. Add the warmed cream and the honey. Use an immersion blender to blend until smooth. Add salt and pepper to taste and keep warm

Make the duck. In a saucepan over medium high heat, reduce the root beer and fig syrup until the mixture is syrupy and coats the back of a spoon. Keep warm.

Pat the skin side of the duck breasts with a dry, clean towel and make 5 to 6 diagonal slits just through skin, being careful not to cut into flesh of the duck. In a dry cast-iron skillet over medium-high heat, sear the duck skin-side first. When the skin is browned and crispy, flip and cook flesh-side until desired doneness (3 to 4 minutes for medium).

Make the green beans. Meanwhile, heat the oil in medium-sized sauté pan over medium heat and sauté the haricot verts for 1 to 2 minutes. Add the Creole seasoning and toss, then shut off the heat and add the honey.

To serve, divide the potatoes among six plates, place 1 duck breast overlapping and drizzle with the fig–root beer glaze over the duck. Add green beans to each plate and garnish with the pecans.

DWAYNE DOMINICK, JR., *TASTE OF LOUISIANA,* **MIXED MEDIA (FOURTH PLACE JUNIOR)**

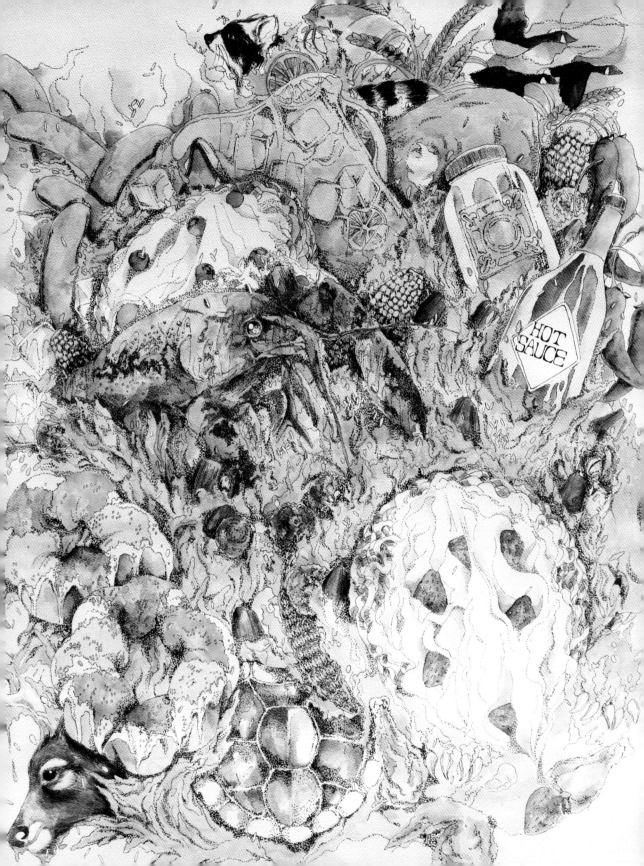

Ville Platte

SERVES 4

FOR THE DUCK:

4 boneless duck breasts, skin on

2½ cups whole milk

2½ cups Coca-Cola

Slap Ya Mama Original Blend Cajun Seasoning, to taste

Slap Ya Mama Cajun Pepper Sauce, to taste

8 slices thick-cut bacon

1 jalapeño pepper, sliced in thin strips (seeded or not, according to taste)

4 ounces cream cheese

FOR THE CHERRY SAUCE:

1 (15-ounce) can black cherries, or 2 cups fresh, pitted

2 cloves garlic, minced

1½ cups chicken stock

1 stem tarragon, minced

STUFFED DUCK BREASTS WRAPPED IN BACON WITH BLACK CHERRY SAUCE
SLAP YA MAMA
WALKER & SONS, OWNERS

Here's another sweet-and-spicy take on duck, this one courtesy of the Walker family. This is a particularly good recipe to use with wild duck, as the marinade will help to remove the gamey taste.

Place the duck breasts in a bowl and pour the milk over them; let marinate for 1 hour. Drain the milk, add the Coca-Cola and let marinate for 1 hour more.

Drain the marinade and pat the duck breasts dry with a paper towel. With a sharp knife cut a small pocket lengthways along the duck breast—be careful not to cut all the way through the breast. Place the duck breasts in a bowl and season generously with Slap Ya Mama Original Blend Cajun Seasoning. Add a few dashes of Slap Ya Mama Cajun Pepper Sauce to the mix. Set aside.

Place your cream cheese in a small microwavable bowl and heat for about 1 minute to help soften the cream cheese. Once your cream cheese is soft, add the thin strips of jalapeño to the bowl and mix. Be sure to coat all the jalapeño strips with cream cheese.

Now take your duck breast and with your fingers place the cream cheese covered jalapeno strips into the pocket you created in the duck breast. Depending on how thick or thin you sliced the jalapenos will determine how many strips you will use to stuff the duck breast.

Once all of your duck breasts have been stuffed it is now time to wrap them in bacon. For each breast lay down 2 slices of bacon side by side. Place 1 duck breast on top of your bacon slices and roll the duck breast and bacon together. To keep the bacon wrapped around the duck, place a toothpick at the end of each bacon slice with the toothpick going all the way through the breast. Continue until all duck breast have been wrapped in bacon.

Grill over medium heat, turning occasionally, for 15 to 30 minutes depending on the thickness of the duck breast. Be sure not to overcook them, as it will dry out the duck breast. Don't forget to remove all toothpicks from the breast before serving.

Drizzle the black cherry sauce over the bacon-wrapped duck breast, or serve it on the side as a dipping sauce.

BLACK CHERRY SAUCE

This goes great with duck and adds a sweetness that pairs well with the spiciness of the jalapeño and Slap Ya Mama seasonings.

With a blender or food processer, blend the black cherries into slush. Pour into a medium saucepan and add the garlic, chicken stock, and tarragon. Bring the mixture to a boil then let simmer and reduce until you have a thick sauce.

BRIANNA DESPENZA, *SAVORING A GOOD TIME*, PENCIL AND GRAPHITE
(TENTH PLACE SENIOR)

SERVES 4

2 Pekin duck

1 cup salt

½ cup shaved garlic

2 cups duck fat

6 sprigs thyme

2 cups Louisiana jasmine rice

1½ cups shelled English peas

1 teaspoon salt

1 teaspoon sugar

4 duck eggs

¼ cup white distilled vinegar

1 tablespoon chopped shallot

1 teaspoon chopped garlic

1 teaspoon turmeric

Salt and freshly ground black pepper, to taste

1 teaspoon chopped thyme

1 tablespoon chopped green onion

CHAPAPEELA DUCK "FRIED RICE"
RESTAURANT AUGUST
JOHN BESH, OWNER
TODD PULSINELLI, EXECUTIVE CHEF

Chapapeela refers to ducks from the Chapapeela Duck Farm in Husser, Louisiana, a favorite source of many of NOLA's top chefs. Like all of John Besh's restaurants, August puts a focus on local ingredients. This recipe also uses the entire duck, from its breast, leg, and eggs, to make a unique twist on Chinese fried rice. Note that the duck leg confit is made at least two days ahead.

Prepare the ducks. Butcher the whole ducks, reserving the breasts and all the excess fat. Place the legs in a bowl, coat with salt and shaved garlic and let cure in the refrigerator for 24 hours. Finely chop the reserved fat and place in a heavy-bottomed saucepan. Heat over medium heat until it's completely rendered, 1 to 2 hours. Strain the fat and refrigerate.

The next day, rinse the salt and garlic mixture from the legs. Place them in a roasting pan, cover with the reserved duck fat and the thyme sprigs. Cover the pan with foil and place into a 200°F oven for 3 hours, or until the meat pulls from bone. Let the meat cool in the fat for 24 hours then pick the meat from the bones.

Make the rice. Rinse the rice in a fine-mesh sieve then place in a medium-sized pot and add 4 cups of water. Bring to a boil and turn off the heat. Cover the pot and let the rice sit for 15 minutes, until cooked through. Fluff the rice and let it cool.

Make the peas. Prepared an ice-water bath in a large bowl. In a medium-sized pan, bring 3 cups of water to a boil and add the salt and sugar. Add the peas and blanch for about 90 seconds then shock them in the ice bath. Set the peas aside.

Poach the duck eggs. In a medium-sized pot, heat 5 cups of water to 188°F (below boiling) and add the distilled vinegar. Crack the eggs into the water and let poach for 3 minutes.

Cook the duck breast. Clean excess fat off the sides of each breast; score the skin with hatch marks. Set a sauté pan over medium heat and let the pan get hot (about 325°F). Salt the duck breasts on both sides and place in the pan skin-side down. Render for 5 minutes on medium to low heat. Flip and cook on the other side for 2 minutes more. Remove from heat and let rest for 4 minutes before slicing.

Finish the dish and plate. In a large sauté pan, sweat the shallots and garlic. Add the rice and toast lightly. Add the chopped thyme, turmeric, and duck confit. Season with salt and pepper, to taste. (Add a little duck fat if the rice is too dry.). Add the peas and divide the rice mixture among four large bowls. Slice each duck breast on the bias and fan the pieces across the top (and to the side) of the rice. With a slotted spoon, pull the duck eggs from the poaching liquid and place in the center of the plate on top of the rice. Garnish with the green onion and serve.

ASHLEIGH MUSCARELLO, *UNTITLED*, **WATERCOLOR**

New Orleans ★

MAKES 6 SERVINGS

1 tablespoon plus
2 teaspoons Chef Paul
Prudhomme's Meat Magic

½ teaspoon ground
nutmeg

2 bay leaves

4 tablespoons unsalted
butter

¾ cup finely chopped
onions

½ cup finely chopped
celery

½ cup finely chopped
green bell peppers

¼ cup finely chopped
green onions

2 teaspoons minced garlic

1 tablespoon Chef Paul
Prudhomme's Magic
Pepper Sauce

1 tablespoon Worcester-
shire sauce

½ cup evaporated milk

½ cup ketchup

1½ pounds ground beef

½ pound ground pork

2 eggs, lightly beaten

1 cup very fine dry breadcrumbs

CHEF PAUL'S MEATLOAF
K-PAUL'S LOUISIANA KITCHEN
PAUL PRUDHOMME, CHEF/OWNER

Chef Paul Prudhomme was already a local legend by the time he and his wife Kay opened K-Paul's Louisiana Kitchen in the heart of the French Quarter in 1979. Since then, he has brought his native Cajun cuisine to the world, popularizing blackened red fish among many traditional dishes. Here is his version of classic meatloaf, Cajun-style.

Combine the Meat Magic, nutmeg, and bay leaves and set aside.

Melt the butter in a 1-quart saucepan over medium heat. Add the onions, celery, bell peppers, green onions, garlic, Magic Pepper Sauce, Worcestershire sauce, and the seasoning mix. Sauté, stirring occasionally and scraping the bottom of the pan, until the mixture starts sticking excessively, about 6 minutes. Stir in the milk and ketchup. Continue cooking for 2 minutes more, stirring occasionally. Remove from the heat and let cool at room temperature. Remove the bay leaves and discard.

Preheat the oven to 350°F. Place the ground meat in an un-greased 13 x 9-inch baking pan. Add the eggs, the cooked veg-etable mixture, and the breadcrumbs. Mix by hand until thor-oughly combined. Shape the mixture into a loaf that is about 12 x 6 x 1½ inches—it will not touch the sides of the pan—and bake uncovered for 25 minutes. Raise the heat to 400°F and continue cooking until done, about 35 minutes more.

PEPPER JELLY–GLAZED BOUDIN MEATLOAF

HOUSE OF BLUES NEW ORLEANS
NATHAN WINOWICH, CHEF

New Orleans

MAKES 2 LOAVES

Great food and great music are the hallmarks of the House of Blues. According to Chef Winowich, this recipe was developed to bring boudin—the Cajun sausage made from pork, rice, and seasoning—to the center of the plate. The chef suggests this meatloaf is best accompanied by mashed potatoes and Cajun boiled Brussels sprouts.

Melt the butter in a sauté pan, and sauté the onions and bell peppers until soft.

Preheat the oven to 375°F. In a large bowl, mix together the pork, boudin, jalapeños, rice, eggs, breadcrumbs, hot sauce, cayenne, paprika, thyme, mustard, and salt. Add the onions and bell peppers and mix well.

Divide the meat mixture between two loaf pans or form into two even rectangular loaves side by side on a rimmed baking sheet and bake for 1 hour, 20 minutes, or until the internal temperature reads 160°F.

Once the meatloaves are in the oven, mix together the ketchup and pepper jelly. After the first 10 minutes in the oven, glaze the loaves with half of the glaze. Re-glaze as needed throughout the baking time. Let the loaves rest for about 20 minutes before serving.

FOR THE MEATLOAF:

1 tablespoon butter

2 cups small diced white onions

1 cup small diced red bell pepper

1 pound ground pork

2 pounds boudin link sausage, removed from its casings

½ cup minced jalapeño peppers

1 cup cooked brown rice

3 eggs

2 cups breadcrumbs

2 tablespoons hot sauce

¼ teaspoon cayenne pepper

1 teaspoon paprika

1 teaspoon dried thyme

1 tablespoons Creole mustard

4 teaspoons salt

FOR THE GLAZE:

1 cup ketchup

1 cup pepper jelly

New Orleans ★

2 (1-pound) cleaned pork tenderloins

4 teaspoons vegetable oil

5½ teaspoons Old Bay Seasoning, divided

4 teaspoons chopped garlic

1 cup fig preserves

2 ounces bourbon whiskey

¼ cup tomato puree

GRILLED PORK TENDERLOIN WITH BOURBON-FIG BARBECUE SAUCE
COMMANDER'S PALACE
TORY MCPHAIL, EXECUTIVE CHEF

Chef McPhail suggests serving this pork cooked just to medium, with a light pink center; otherwise you risk a dry and chewy roast. The restaurant serves this deliciously rich dish with cracked corn grits and ripped arugula.

Place the pork on a rimmed baking sheet and season with the oil, 4 teaspoons of the Old Bay Seasoning, and the garlic. Rub the mixture onto all sides of the meat, set it aside and fire up the grill.

For the barbecue sauce, combine the fig preserves, bourbon, tomato puree, and the remaining 1½ teaspoons Old Bay Seasoning with ½ cup water in a bowl and mix with a spoon. You may need to adjust the consistency of the sauce with more water depending on the thickness of the preserves.

Grill the pork over medium to low heat until it is cooked to your desired temperature, usually 5 to 8 minutes. Glaze the pork with the barbecue sauce for the final 2 minutes of cooking.

Slice the pork into ½-inch thick medallions and serve.

ELIZABETH WALKER, *FRENCH PRESSED*, OIL AND ACRYLIC

New Orleans ★

SERVES 6 TO 8

FOR THE PORK:

1 (4-pound) Boston butt pork roast, sliced into 1-inch thick cutlets

Salt and freshly ground black pepper, to taste

2 cups all-purpose flour

1 teaspoon Creole seasoning

¼ cup rendered bacon fat

1 large onion, diced small

1 rib celery, diced small

½ bell pepper, diced small

2 cloves garlic, minced

2 cups diced tomatoes

2 cups beef stock

1 sprig thyme, picked

1 teaspoon crushed red pepper flakes

1 bay leaf

1 tablespoon Worcester-shire sauce

2 green onions, chopped

Tabasco sauce, to taste

SLOW-COOKED PORK GRILLADES AND GRITS
MOPHO
MICHAEL GULOTTA, CHEF

"This was my grandmother Doris's favorite dish," says Chef Gulotta, a New Orleans native. "In my house it was always a dish made for any kind of special occasion because everyone requested it for their birthdays, or for Mardi Gras, and so on. From there it became everyone's favorite dish. My family always does it with veal top round or even beef top round. But I started doing it with pork because it's so tender and just falls apart."

Season the pork cutlets with salt and black pepper and season the flour with the Creole seasoning. In a large frying pan, heat the bacon fat on high. Dredge the pork in the flour and add to the pan in batches. (Don't throw out the flour.)

Cook the cutlets on both sides until golden brown, being careful not to overcrowd the pan. Once all of the pork has browned, add the onion to the pan and lower the heat to medium high. Sweat the onions until they become a deep mahogany color then add the celery, bell pepper, and garlic.

Continue cooking the vegetables while constantly stirring on medium for 5 minutes. Add a tablespoon of the leftover seasoned flour to the pan and whisk so that no lumps exist.

Add the tomatoes and beef stock while stirring and raise heat to high until the liquid comes to a boil. Reduce the heat to a simmer and add the thyme, red pepper flakes, bay leaf, Worcestershire, and the pork cutlets back to the pan and continue simmering for 45 minutes or until the meat is fork tender.

Season the pork grillades to taste with salt, pepper, and Tabasco and serve over creamy Jalapeño Cheese Grits.

JALEPEÑO CHEESE GRITS

Preheat the oven to 400°F.

In a saucepan over high heat bring 4 cups of water to a boil while slowly whisking in the stone-ground grits. Reduce the heat to medium low and cover the pot. Let the grits slowly cook for 20 minutes.

While the grits are cooking, roast the jalapeño pepper in the oven for 10 minutes so that the skin blisters and can be easily removed. Cut the pepper in half lengthwise and, holding it under cold running water, remove the skin and the seeds. Place the pepper on a cutting board and mince and add it to the pot of grits.

Remove the grits from the flame and fold in the butter, mascarpone and Edam cheeses.

Season with salt to taste and serve.

FOR THE CHEESE GRITS:

SERVES 6 TO 8

1 cup stone-ground white corn grits

1 jalapeño pepper

3 tablespoons butter

2 tablespoons mascarpone or cream cheese

¼ cup grated Edam cheese

Salt, to taste

BROOKE BOURGEOIS, *ROUX*, OIL AND ACRYLIC (SIXTH PLACE SENIOR)

CAJUN-FRIED PORK CHOPS

SLAP YA MAMA

WALKER & SONS, OWNERS

Fish fry isn't just for fish. Here, it makes a great crunchy coating for pork chops. If you would like for your pork chops to be a little spicier, add some Slap Ya Mama Cajun Seasoning to the fish-fry mix or shake it onto the cooked chops. French fries make an excellent side dish.

Coat the bottom of a frying pan with a light layer of vegetable oil and heat on high. Pour the Slap Ya Mama Fish Fry into a shallow pan. Rinse each pork chop under cold water and shake off excess water. Place each pork chop in the pan of Fish Fry and roll until they are evenly coated.

Once your oil is hot, reduce the heat to medium-high and place the pork chops in the pan. Working in batches, cook until golden brown on both sides, flipping each pork chop as it cooks. Place cooked pork chops on absorbent paper and serve hot.

Ville Platte

SERVES 4

2 tablespoons vegetable oil

8 boneless pork chops, ¼-inch thick

1 cup Slap Ya Mama Cajun Fish Fry

ALEXANDER RICHARDSON, *GUMBO JAZZ*, MIXED MEDIA (FIFTH PLACE SENIOR)

Monroe ★

MAKES 8 SANDWICHES

FOR THE RABBIT:

½ cup all-purpose flour

1½ teaspoons salt

½ teaspoon freshly ground white pepper

1¼ teaspoons cayenne pepper

½ cup yellow cornmeal

½ cup cornstarch

2 tablespoons canola or vegetable oil

1 egg, slightly beaten

1¼ teaspoons baking powder

8 rabbit loins, divided into 2-ounce portions

Salt and freshly ground black pepper

Light colored oil for frying

FOR THE ONION GRAVY:

6 tablespoons butter

4 cups yellow onion, thinly sliced

4 tablespoons all-purpose flour

¼ cup apple cider vinegar

3 cups chicken stock

2 tablespoons salt

(Continued)

CHICKEN FRIED RABBIT PO' BOY
COTTON RESTAURANT
CORY BAHR, CHEF

Monroe native son Cory Bahr has a national reputation for seafood and an inventive take on classic Southern dishes. Here he turns Louisiana's famous Po' Boy sandwich on its head with fried rabbit and a savory onion gravy. No messing with the bread though—the Leidenheimer French bread recommended by Chef Bahr is considered an essential component. The Leidenheimer Baking Company has been family owned and operated in New Orleans since 1896.

Make the rabbit. Season the flour with salt, pepper, and cayenne. Measure out ¼ cup and set it aside. Combine the remaining flour with 1 cup cold water, the cornmeal, cornstarch, oil, egg, and baking powder to form a tempura batter.

Season the rabbit loins with salt and pepper. Pat dry. Lightly coat in the reserved flour, shaking off any excess. Lightly dip into the cornmeal tempura batter, shaking off any excess.

Heat 3 inches of frying oil in a heavy-bottomed skillet until the oil reaches 300°F. Fry the rabbit until it floats to the surface plus 1 additional minute, turning once.

Make the gravy. Heat the butter in a saucepan, add the onions and sauté until the onions are caramelized. Stir in the flour. Mix together the vinegar and stock, and add to the pan.

Bring up heat slightly and cook 3 to 5 minutes more, until the gravy is thick and flour taste has cooked out. Season with the salt and thyme.

Assemble the Po' Boys. Layer the lettuce, tomatoes, mayonnaise, and mustard on bread. Add sliced fried rabbit and top with caramelized onion gravy.

BALDWIN BIOG, *LOUISIANA BRANDED,* MIXED MEDIA (DETAIL)

2 tablespoons thyme,
leaves picked off and
roughly chopped

FOR THE PO' BOYS:

8 loaves Leidenheimer
French Bread, split and
toasted

1 head Boston lettuce

3 Creole tomatoes, sliced
¼-inch thick

½ cup mayonnaise

½ cup Creole mustard

Lacombe ★

SERVES 6

FOR THE RABBIT SAUSAGE:

2 eggs, beaten

1 cup milk

1 cup panko breadcrumbs

1 shallot, minced

5 cloves garlic, minced

2 tablespoons olive oil

5 pounds rabbit meat, diced large and half frozen

1 pound pork fatback, cut into strips

2 tablespoons fennel seed, toasted and ground

1 tablespoon fennel seed, ground

4 tablespoons garlic powder

4 teaspoons onion powder

2 teaspoons freshly ground black pepper

1 tablespoon red crushed pepper

1 tablespoon dried oregano

1 teaspoon sugar

2 tablespoons salt

RAGOUT OF ITALIAN RABBIT SAUSAGE AND RICOTTA CAVATELLI
LA PROVENCE
JOHN BESH, OWNER/ERICK LOOS, CHEF DE CUISINE

More than 40 years ago, legendary chef Chris Kerageorgiou established La Provence on the northeastern edge of Lake Pontchartrain. Among the many chefs mentored by Chef Kerageorgiou was young John Besh. In 2007, Besh purchased the restaurant from his ailing mentor and extended the small kitchen garden to encompass a sustainable farm. With the installation of Erick Loos as chef de cuisine, Besh continues the mentor/mentee tradition.

In describing this dish, Chef Loos says: "Rabbit is something special here at La Provence. John taught me to cook rabbit at a young age at Restaurant August when I had just begun to learn the traditions and history of Louisiana cooking. Just as Chef Chris taught John here at La Provence when he was my age, we would slow-braise rabbit with lots of onions, garlic, orange peel, chili flakes, and fresh herbs then serve it over handmade pasta. The rabbit would almost take the consistency of a stew, falling off of the bone, and we would always serve it with fresh crusty French bread. This is another take on the dish we used to cook together."

Make the rabbit sausage. In a small bowl, whisk the eggs, add in the milk and panko, then place in the refrigerator to use later.

Sauté the shallot and garlic in olive oil until light brown and transparent then lay them on a plate in the freezer. This will be used to grind with the meat later. Toss the rabbit meat and fatback together with the toasted fennel seed, ground fennel seed, garlic powder, onion powder, black pepper, red crushed pepper, oregano, sugar and salt.

Grind the mix through the coarse die of a meat grinder twice, making sure the meat stays below 40°F. Place half of the meat mixture in a food processor and pulse several times; the meat will smooth out a little.

Place the meat mixture and the egg-panko mixture in the bowl of a stand mixer fitted with the paddle attachment. Mix on medium speed for 2 minutes, check, and adjust the seasoning if necessary. Hold the sausage mixture in the refrigerator for later use.

Make the cavatelli. Mix the eggs and ricotta in a food processor then add the Parmigiano, flour, and salt at once. Pulse until the dough crumbles and distributes evenly. Pour the crumbly dough mixture onto your work surface and press and knead into a ball. Let the dough rest in the refrigerator for 1 hour.

Roll into ½-inch ropes and work through a cavatelli wheel (see Note) while keeping the pasta lightly floured. Blanch the cavatelli for 3 minutes in lightly salted water and drain. Toss with olive oil to coat. Hold for later use.

Make the ragout. Add the olive oil to a sauté pan over medium-high heat. Add in the mushrooms and let them sauté until golden brown on the outside. Add in the shallot, garlic, thyme, and crushed red pepper and cook just for a second, until the aroma fills the air. Add in the chicken stock and butter and bring to a simmer.

Brown the sausage mixture in a large saucepot on medium heat until almost done (just a little pink left in the middle). Pour the ragout over the sausage and add in the cherry tomatoes. Adjust the consistency with more chicken stock if needed. Add in the pasta and bring to a simmer then portion into your entrée bowls. Check for and adjust salt as needed. Garnish with the fresh shaved Parmigiano cheese.

Note: A cavatelli wheel is a hand-cranked pasta roller that will shape the pasta and mark it with the characteristic ridges.

FOR THE CAVATELLI PASTA:

2 eggs

5 ounces fresh ricotta

2 ounces Parmigiano-Reggiano, grated

1 pound all-purpose flour

Pinch of salt

Splash of olive oil

FOR THE RAGOUT OF CHANTERELLE MUSHROOMS:

2 tablespoons extra virgin olive oil

1 pound fresh chanterelle mushrooms, rinsed and cleaned

1 shallot, minced

2 cloves garlic, minced

1 tablespoon thyme leaves, picked and chopped

Pinch of crushed red pepper

2 cups chicken stock, plus more as needed

2 tablespoons butter

1 cup cherry tomatoes

Salt to taste

A few shavings of fresh Parmigiano-Reggiano, for garnish

3 tablespoons vegetable oil, divided

1 tablespoon salt

¾ pound fresh fettuccini, or ½ pound dry

2 sticks (½ pound) unsalted butter

2½ cups heavy cream

2 tablespoons Chef Paul Prudhomme's Pork and Veal Magic or Vegetable Magic, or 1 tablespoon plus 2 teaspoons Meat Magic, divided

¾ cup plus 4 teaspoons finely grated Parmesan cheese, divided

1¾ cups very fine dry breadcrumbs

1½ tablespoons minced fresh parsley

1½ tablespoons olive oil

3 eggs

6 (3½- to 4-ounce) slices baby white veal, pounded thin

Vegetable oil for pan-frying

PANEED VEAL AND FETTUCCINI
K-PAUL'S LOUISIANA KITCHEN
PAUL PRUDHOMME, CHEF/OWNER

Paneed is just a south Louisiana term for quick pan-frying. Chef Prudhomme recommends this method for thin pieces of many kinds of meat, as it preserves the flavor of the meat while still cooking it thoroughly. It works particularly well with a mild meat like veal, which in this recipe is enhanced with just the right amount of seasoning and combined with tender pasta.

Add 4 quarts of water, 2 tablespoons of the oil, and the salt to a large pot over high heat. Cover and bring to a rolling boil. Add the fettuccini in small amounts at a time, breaking up the oil patches as you drop it in. Return to a boil and cook to al dente stage (about 3 minutes if using fresh pasta, 7 minutes if dry), but do not overcook. During this cooking time, use a wooden or spaghetti spoon to lift the fettuccini out of the water by spoonfuls and shake strands back into the boiling water (a procedure that seems to enhance the pasta's texture).

Immediately drain the fettuccini in a colander and stop its cooking by running cold water over the strands. (If you use dry pasta, first rinse with hot water to wash off excess starch.) After the pasta has cooled thoroughly, about 2 to 3 minutes, pour the remaining 1 tablespoon of vegetable oil in your hands and gently rub the fettuccini until it's well coated with oil. Set aside, still in the colander.

Melt the butter in a large skillet over medium-low heat. Add the cream and 1 teaspoon of the Pork and Veal Magic (or other Magic Seasoning Blend), and turn the heat to medium-high. Whisk the mixture constantly as it comes to a boil, then reduce the heat and simmer, still whisking constantly, until the sauce has reduced some and thickened enough to coat a spoon well, about 7 to 8 minutes. Remove from the heat, gradually add ¾ cup of the Parmesan, whisking until the cheese melts, and set aside.

Combine the breadcrumbs, parsley, olive oil and remaining Pork and Veal Magic (or other Magic Seasoning Blend) in a shallow baking pan. Beat the eggs in a separate shallow pan, then beat in the remaining 4 teaspoons Parmesan. Soak the veal in the egg mixture for at least 5 minutes, being sure to coat it thoroughly.

Meanwhile, heat ¼-inch oil to about 400°F in a large skillet. Then, just before frying, dredge the veal in the seasoned bread-crumbs, coating well and pressing the crumbs in with your hands. Shake off any excess. Fry the veal in the hot oil until golden brown, about 1 minute per side. Do not crowd. If any of the crumbs in the bottom start to burn, change the oil immediately. Remove the veal to a large platter and set aside.

Reheat the cheese sauce over medium-high heat, whisking frequently. If the butter starts to separate, whisk in 1 tablespoon of cream or water. Add the fettuccini and toss until thoroughly coated and heated through, about 1 minute. Remove from the heat and serve immediately.

To serve, place a piece of veal on each heated serving plate. Roll each portion of fettuccini onto a large fork and slide onto the plate. Top with additional sauce from the skillet.

SEAN HICKS, *LAISSEZ LES BON TEMPS ROULER*, OIL AND ACRYLIC

Lafayette
★

SERVES 2

FOR THE GRITS:

1 cup whole milk

2 tablespoons butter

¼ cup grits

FOR THE GRILLADES:

½ cup olive oil, divided

2 (4-ounce) veal medallions

¾ cup all-purpose flour, divided

3 tablespoons diced onion,

3 tablespoons diced celery

2 tablespoon diced green bell pepper

1 teaspoon minced garlic

1 cup chicken stock

1 tablespoon Worcester-shire sauce

1 tablespoon Tiger Sauce

1 tablespoon Kitchen Bouquet

Salt and freshly ground black pepper, to taste

¼ cup sliced green onions, for garnish

¼ cup finely chopped parsley, for garnish

VEAL GRILLADES AND GRITS
CHARLEY G'S
HOLLY GOETTING, CHEF

Chef Goetting's food is driven by Southern inspiration and that's certainly the case with this dish, which has been on the restaurant's luncheon special menu for at least ten years. She describes it as "One of our favorites, especially on a cold day." Tiger Sauce is a sweet-hot vinegar-based pepper sauce. Look for it at national retailers or order online.

Make the grits. In a saucepan, bring the milk and butter to a boil and whisk in the grits. Reduce heat and simmer for about 5 minutes, or until smooth. Set aside.

Make the grillades: In a medium sauté pan heat ¼ cup of the olive oil. Dust the veal medallions with ¼ cup of the flour. Cook in a skillet on medium-high heat for about 3 minutes on each side. Take the veal out of the pan and set aside.

In the same pan, add the remaining ¼ cup olive oil and sauté the onion, celery, bell pepper, and garlic for about 3 minutes. Then add the chicken stock, Worcestershire sauce, Tiger Sauce, Kitchen Bouquet, and salt and pepper. Return the veal to the pan and let simmer for 5 to 10 minutes.

To serve, spoon the veal and sauce over a pile of creamy grits and garnish with the green onions and parsley.

VEAL CHOP JILL
ANDREA'S RESTAURANT
ANDREA APUZZO, CHEF/OWNER

Frequently ranked among the country's top Italian restaurants, Chef Apuzzo opened Andrea's after 35 years of cooking in kitchens all over the world. The richness of this butterflied veal chop is perfectly balanced by the tangy arugula salad topped with uncooked fresh tomato sauce.

Preheat the oven to 425°F. Slicing down with a knife, butterfly the chops. Spread the "wings" on either side and pound out until very thin. Coat with flour, shaking off any excess, and season with salt and pepper. Heat the vegetable oil in a skillet and spread out each veal chop to brown, turning once, about 3 minutes in all. Set on a baking sheet and finish cooking in the hot oven.

Meanwhile, prepare the uncooked sauce by combining the tomatoes, capers, red onion, olive oil, white wine, lemon juice, basil oregano, parsley, salt, and crushed red pepper in a mixing bowl.

To serve, top each veal chop with the arugula, and then spoon on the sauce. Garnish with lemon halves and a drizzle of olive oil.

Metairie

SERVES 2

2 (12- to 14-ounce) veal chops, on the bone

½ cup all-purpose flour

Salt and freshly ground black pepper, to taste

⅓ cup vegetable oil

3 Roma tomatoes, roughly chopped

⅓ cup capers

¼ cup chopped red onion

⅓ cup extra-virgin olive oil

⅓ cup white wine

Juice of 1 lemon (about 3 tablespoons)

1 tablespoon chopped fresh basil

1 tablespoon chopped fresh oregano

1 tablespoon chopped fresh Italian (flat-leaf) parsley

½ teaspoon salt

¼ teaspoon crushed red pepper

2 cups arugula

Lemon halves, for serving

Extra virgin olive oil, for serving

Shreveport

SERVES 4

FOR THE VEAL:

8 (2½ ounce, ⅛-inch thick) veal cutlets

¼ pound provolone cheese

¼ pound mozzarella cheese

16 slices prosciutto

1 cup Italian breadcrumbs

2 teaspoons salt, divided

¾ teaspoon freshly ground black pepper, divided

1¼ teaspoon Ernest's Special Spice, divided (optional, see Note)

1 cup all-purpose flour

3 large eggs

2 tablespoons unsalted butter

3 tablespoons olive oil

VEAL CORDON BLEU WITH CHAMPAGNE SAUCE
ERNEST'S ORLEANS RESTAURANT
ERNEST PALMISANO, JR., OWNER/CHEF

Underscoring the fact that Ernest's is a family owned and operated restaurant—and has been so for more than 60 years—this Italian version of the classic Veal Cordon Bleu is Tina Palmisano's recipe.

If cutlets are thicker than ⅛ inch, pound them between sheets of plastic wrap with flat side of meat pounder. Using a cheese plane, shave enough provolone and mozzarella cheese to make a layer of each cheese for each of 4 cutlets.

Pat dry 2 cutlets of the same shape and arrange 1 cutlet on a work surface. Put 2 slices of prosciutto on the cutlet, leaving a ¼-inch border of veal around the prosciutto. Add a layer of provolone, top with another layer of prosciutto, add a layer of mozzarella, then place the second cutlet on top of the cheese. Lightly pound the ¼-inch border around the cutlets' outer edges to seal the veal sandwich. Make 3 more sandwiches in same manner.

Set a rack over a baking sheet and set aside. Line another baking sheet with wax paper and set out three large shallow baking dishes on top for a breading station. In the first dish, stir together the breadcrumbs, 1 teaspoon of the salt, and ¼ teaspoon of the pepper. In the second dish, stir together the flour, 1 teaspoon of Ernest's Special Spice, ¾ teaspoon of the salt, and ¼ teaspoon of the pepper. In the third, whisk together the eggs, the remaining ¼ teaspoon salt, ¼ teaspoon pepper, and ¼ teaspoon Ernest's Special Spice.

Dredge 1 veal sandwich in the flour, knocking off excess, then dip in the egg to coat, letting excess drip off, and finally dredge in the breadcrumbs, patting to help them adhere. Set the breaded sandwich on the rack set on a baking sheet and coat the remaining sandwiches in same manner. Chill, uncovered, for 1 hour, and let stand at room temperature 30 minutes before cooking.

When ready to cook, heat 1 tablespoon of the butter and 1½ tablespoons of the oil in a 12-inch heavy skillet over moderately high heat until foam subsides. Add 2 veal sandwiches, then reduce heat to moderate and cook, turning over once, until golden, about 4 minutes total. Transfer to plates and wipe out skillet with paper towels. Cook remaining sandwiches in remaining butter and oil in same manner. Serve with Champagne sauce.

Note: Ernest's Special Spice is a Mediterranean-Creole blend that is the restaurant's house seasoning. It can be ordered by calling or emailing the restaurant.

CHAMPAGNE SAUCE

Add the stock and dried mushrooms to a medium-sized pot. Cover and bring to a boil, then reduce heat to its lowest setting.

In another medium-sized pot, add the Champagne and shallots. Bring to a rolling boil, and continue to cook until the wine has reduced to ¾ cup. Turn off the heat and wait until the wine stops simmering, then whisk in ¼ cup of the butter, a little at a time.

Heat the remaining 3 tablespoons butter in a saucepan over medium-high heat. When the butter stops foaming, add the flour and stir well to combine. Stirring often, cook this roux for 5 minutes, or until it turns the color of coffee-with-cream.

Pour the Champagne sauce into the roux and stir until smooth. Strain the reconstituted mushrooms and fold them into the sauce.

LAUREN NASSOUR, *FESTIVE AIR,* OIL AND ACRYLIC

FOR THE CHAMPAGNE SAUCE:

1 cup chicken or vegetable stock

½ ounce dried porcini mushrooms (or other dried mushrooms)

2 cups Champagne or sparkling wine

⅓ cup minced shallots

¼ cup plus 3 tablespoons unsalted butter, divided

3 tablespoons all-purpose flour

Salt, to taste

Monroe ★

SERVES 4

½ pound angel hair pasta

2 tablespoons extra virgin olive oil

2½ teaspoons salt

1¾ teaspoons freshly ground black pepper

3 tablespoons plus 1 teaspoon chopped fresh parsley

2 teaspoons chopped fresh basil

2 teaspoons freshly grated Parmesan cheese

2 cups all-purpose flour

8 (2½- to 3-ounce) veal medallions, pounded ¼-inch thick

2 tablespoons olive oil

3 tablespoons unsalted butter

½ cup dry white wine

¼ cup chicken stock or canned low-sodium chicken broth

2 tablespoons fresh lemon juice

2 tablespoons capers, drained

2 tablespoons minced garlic

VEAL PICCATA WITH ANGEL HAIR
BACCO ITALIAN GRILLE
CHAD MATRANA, CHEF

Bacco Italian Grille is part of the revitalization of downtown Monroe. Chef Matrana, a New Orleans native, serves a mix of Mediterranean favorites, from pizza to classics like this one.

Bring a large pot of salted water to a boil. Add the pasta and cook, stirring to separate the strands, until just al dente, about 4 minutes. Drain in a colander and return to the pot. Add the extra virgin olive oil, ½ teaspoon of the salt, ¼ teaspoon of the pepper, 2 tablespoons of the parsley, the basil, and Parmesan and toss to coat. Cover to keep warm.

Meanwhile, combine the flour with 1 teaspoon of the salt and 1 teaspoon of the black pepper in a shallow bowl.

Lightly season both sides of each medallion with the remaining salt and pepper. One at a time, dredge the medallions in the seasoned flour, shaking to remove any excess.

Heat the olive oil and melt 1 tablespoon of the butter in a large skillet or sauté pan over medium heat. Add the medallions in batches and cook until golden brown and cooked through, 1 to 1½ minutes per side. Drain on paper towels and set aside.

Add the wine to the juices remaining in the pan and bring to a boil, stirring to deglaze the pan. Cook until the wine is reduced by half, 2 to 3 minutes. Add the chicken stock, lemon juice, capers, and garlic and return to a boil, stirring until the mixture is thickened, about 4 minutes. Stir in the remaining 2 tablespoons of butter and 1 tablespoon of parsley. When the butter is melted, return the veal medallions to the pan and cook until heated through, about 1 minute.

To serve, divide the pasta among four large plates, and arrange two veal medallions on each. Spoon the sauce over the veal and garnish each serving with the remaining parsley. Serve immediately.

COMMUNITY COFFEE MARINATED RACK OF LAMB

LATIL'S LANDING RESTAURANT AT HOUMAS HOUSE PLANTATION

JEREMY LANGLOIS, EXECUTIVE CHEF

Darrow ★

SERVES 4

4 (4-bone) racks of lamb, frenched

5 cups brewed Community Coffee, chilled

Salt and freshly ground black pepper, to taste

2 tablespoons olive oil

Latil's Landing, one of four restaurants that dot this plantation estate, is located in the French House, built in the 1770s by Alexander Latil. This elegant rack of lamb is well-suited to the restaurant's ambiance. According to Chef Langlois, "Community Coffee is a Baton Rouge–based company, and is the largest family-owned coffee company in America. It is one of the true flavors of the south and surprisingly, using it as a marinade for lamb enhances with subtle flavors of the meat." Note that the lamb is marinated up to 24 hours before cooking. Ask your butcher to "french," or clean, the bones.

Place the racks of lamb in a container and completely cover with the Community Coffee. Marinate in the refrigerator between 12 and 24 hours.

Preheat the oven to 400°F. Remove the lamb from the marinade and pat dry with a paper towel. Season the lamb generously with salt and pepper.

Heat a large sauté pan over high heat and add the olive oil. Sauté the lamb on each side until the meat is golden brown. Place in a roasting pan and cook in the oven until the internal temperature is 130°F, about 12 minutes. Remove the lamb from the oven and allow the meat to rest on a cutting board for 10 minutes. Slice the meat between the bones into chops and serve.

New Orleans
★

SERVES 4

2 sticks (¼ pound) un-salted butter, softened, divided

8 (2½-ounce) scallops of beef tenderloin

1 teaspoon Creole meat seasoning

½ cup demi-glace (see Note)

2 teaspoons currant jelly

¼ cup port

BEEF TENDERLOIN WITH TCHOUPITOULAS SAUCE
COMMANDER'S PALACE
TORY McPHAIL, EXECUTIVE CHEF

Named after an old Louisiana Mardi Gras Indian tribe and a well-known New Orleans street, this new beef dish is light and very elegant. If you have the demi-glace on hand, it can be prepared in minutes. You can also substitute medallions of veal or double veal chops.

Heat a cast-iron skillet until very hot. Add 1 stick of the butter. Season the meat with the Creole seasoning and sauté quickly on both sides, turning only once, until cooked to desired degree of doneness. Remove to warm platter and keep warm.

Add the demi-glace, jelly, and port to the butter and juices remaining in skillet. Cook, stirring in all the bits of glaze from bottom and sides of pan, until the sauce is reduced by half. Add the remaining butter and swirl pan over heat until butter is just melted and the sauce has a translucent glaze. Do not let it boil. Pour the sauce over the beef and serve immediately.

Note: Demi-glace is a rich, greatly reduced combination of espagnole sauce (in itself a highly reduced seasoned brown sauce), brown stock, and Madeira. Making it at home is labor-intensive, but you can purchase ready-made demi-glace in gourmet specialty shops and online.

ALEX HOPE ROSENZWEIG, *CLEAN UP AT 3AM,* OIL AND ACRYLIC (THIRD PLACE SENIOR)

CHAPTER FOUR

FISH AND SEAFOOD

Metairie

1 tablespoon olive oil

1 teaspoon chopped garlic

½ cup small diced celery

½ cup small diced onion

½ cup small diced green
bell pepper

½ of 1 bay leaf

1 teaspoon fresh thyme,
divided

4 cups Louisiana shrimp,
crab, or fish stock, divided

1 pound Gulf redfish fillets

1 teaspoon Creole seasoning

2½ cups chopped fresh
tomatoes

1 teaspoon chopped
parsley

Pinch of freshly ground
black pepper

Salt, to taste

½ cup brown rice

1 cup stock or water

Pinch of salt

Thinly sliced green onions,
for garnish

LOW-FAT REDFISH COURTBOUILLON
HERITAGE GRILL BY RALPH BRENNAN
STEVEN MARSELLA, EXECUTIVE CHEF

New American Creole Cuisine is the hallmark of this lunch-only member of the Ralph Brennan Restaurant Group. Chef Marsella presents his lighter take on classic dishes, as shown here, where a very small amount of olive oil replaces the usual butter.

Heat the olive oil in a deep skillet; add the garlic and cook until it turns a golden color. Add the celery, onion, bell pepper, bay leaf, ½ teaspoon of the thyme, and 1 cup of the stock. Simmer until the liquid evaporates. Stir in the tomatoes, add 2 cups of the stock and simmer for about 15 minutes on low heat.

While the courtbouillon is simmering, season the redfish fillets with Creole seasoning. Heat a nonstick skillet over medium-high heat, spray with canola cooking spray and place the fillets in skillet, seasoned-side down. Sear for about 2 minutes until fillets start to brown. Remove fillets and set aside.

After the courtbouillon has simmered for 15 minutes, add the fish fillets, the remaining 1 cup stock, the parsley and the remaining ½ teaspoon thyme. Cover, reduce heat, and slowly simmer for 8 to 10 minutes.

Make the rice. Place the rice in a mesh strainer and rinse under cold water for 30 seconds. Combine the rice, stock, and salt in a saucepot. Bring to a boil, cover, and reduce heat to low. Cook until the liquid has been absorbed, about 20 minutes. Remove from heat, uncover, and fluff with a fork.

To serve, place rice in a shallow bowl, remove fish fillets and place on top of rice. Pour courtbouillon around the rice and over the fish. Garnish with thinly sliced green onions.

KRIS KALUBA, *VOODOO STU*, MIXED MEDIA (SEVENTH PLACE SENIOR)

New Orleans ★

SERVES 6

FOR THE REDFISH:

Vegetable oil for brushing the grill rack and fish fillets (do not use olive oil)

6 (6- to 8-ounce) Louisiana redfish fillets with skin and scales still attached on one side, neatly trimmed, including removing the "belly" if still attached

1 tablespoon Creole seasoning

2 to 3 tablespoons of dry white wine, if grilling in batches

FOR THE MÂITRE D'HÔTEL BUTTER:

½ cup (1 stick) unsalted butter, left at room temperature until very soft

2 tablespoons minced thyme leaves

2 tablespoons minced Italian (flat-leaf) parsley leaves

1 tablespoon freshly squeezed lemon juice

1½ teaspoons minced shallots

(*Continued*)

GRILLED REDFISH "ON THE HALF-SHELL" WITH MAITRE D'HÔTEL BUTTER
RALPH BRENNAN'S RED FISH GRILL
AUSTIN KIRZNER, EXECUTIVE CHEF

This French Quarter flagship of Ralph Brennan's family of restaurants is a veritable palace of Gulf seafood, as you might expect from the man who wrote the book on how to cook it. Of course you'll find many versions of the restaurant's namesake on the menu, including this one, in which the popular redfish is simply grilled and flavorfully served.

Clean the grill rack with a wire brush and preheat it until it is hot. Then add wet or dry hickory, or other wood chips. Brush the rack with a thick wad of paper towels saturated in salad oil, holding the paper towels with long-handled tongs so you don't burn yourself.

Place the fillets skin-side down on a work surface. Make sure the skinless sides are free of any loose scales. Brush the skinless sides with the oil, and season each fillet evenly on the skinless side with ½ teaspoon of the Creole seasoning.

Once the grill is ready, place the fillets directly on it, skin-side down, and cook until they are done, 5 to 8 minutes. The cooking time will vary according to the heat of the grill and the thickness of the fillets. (Watch closely so the fish does not overcook.) Do not turn the fillets over. Use a broad, large and sturdy spatula to lift each fillet from the grill at least once while cooking so it doesn't stick excessively. To test for doneness, insert the tip of a knife into the thickest part of a fillet to separate the flesh a little to assess if it's cooked all the way through.

If cooking the fillets in batches, transfer the cooked fillets, skin-side down, to a heat-proof platter placed in a warm spot, and drizzle the fillets with white wine to keep them moist while grilling the remaining fish.

Once all the fillets are cooked, serve immediately, skin-side down on heated dinner plates. Top the fillets with rounds of mâitre d'hôtel butter, using a total of 1 to 1½ tablespoons of butter for each serving

MÂITRE D'HÔTEL BUTTER

Combine all ingredients together in a medium-size mixing bowl, whisking until well blended.

Use immediately, or roll in waxed or parchment paper into a log that is about 5-inches long and 1¼ inches in diameter, then wrap the log snugly in plastic wrap. The butter will keep in the refrigerator for up to 2 weeks, or frozen for up to 2 months.

1 teaspoon minced garlic

¼ teaspoon kosher salt

Pinch of freshly ground black pepper

CHARLOTTE CHAUVIN, *CULTURAL FUSION*, OIL AND ACRYLIC

Baton Rouge
★

FOR THE WHITE BEANS:

4 tablespoons olive oil

2 cloves garlic, chopped

1 shallot, chopped

2 roasted red peppers, chopped

4 basil leaves, chopped

1 tablespoon herbed butter (see Note)

Salt and freshly ground black pepper, to taste

¼ cup white wine

4 (15.5-ounce) cans white navy beans, rinsed

FOR THE PANEED REDFISH:

1½ to 2 cups all-purpose flour

Salt and freshly ground black pepper, to taste

¼ cup olive oil

10 (5- to 7-ounce) Louisiana redfish filets

2 tablespoons butter, optional

Juice of ½ lemon (1½ tablespoons)

PANEED LOUISIANA REDFISH ON A SAUTÉ OF WHITE BEANS
STROUBES SEAFOOD AND STEAKS
SCOTT VARNEDOE, EXECUTIVE CHEF

The classic Louisiana preparation of the classic Louisiana fish, this recipe took first place in a recent Louisiana Seafood competition. The fish is served with a flavorful side of white beans and topped with brown butter sauce.

Make the beans. In a large sauté pan heat the olive oil and sauté the garlic and shallots. When garlic is just about to toast, add the red peppers, basil, herbed butter, salt and pepper, the white wine, and the beans. Heat through. Keep hot until needed.

Cook the fish. Place the flour in a shallow dish and season with salt and pepper. In a medium sauté pan, heat the oil until very hot. Working in batches, coat the fish with the seasoned flour, knock off excess, and add the fish to the pan. Cook for 2 minutes and flip. Cook for 3 minutes more. Add the butter and lemon to the pan and coat the fish. Keep hot until needed.

Make the sauce. In a medium saucepan over medium heat, melt the butter and cook until an amber color and nutty aroma is achieved. Add the sundried tomatoes, capers, lemon juice and salt and pepper and heat through.

To serve, place a mound of the white beans on each of 10 large plates. Top with the fish and drizzle with the sauce. Top with some pickled onions and fennel and a touch of fresh parmesan cheese.

Note: Herbed butter is a great staple to keep in your freezer. In the bowl of a stand mixer fitted with the paddle attachment, combine ½ pound room temperature unsalted butter with 1 teaspoon kosher salt, ¼ teaspoon freshly ground black pepper, ¼ teaspoon minced garlic, 1 tablespoon minced Italian (flat-leaf) parsley, 2 teaspoons lemon zest, and 2 teaspoons each of the herbs of your choice. (This is a great way to use up leftover fresh herbs.) Beat until mixed thoroughly, but do not whip. Lay the

ELIZABETH ROTHERMEL, *BLACKENED REDFISH HURRICANE,* WATERCOLOR

butter out onto waxed or parchment paper and roll into a log. Wrap in plastic and keep it in the refrigerator for 2 weeks, or up to 2 months in the freezer.

FOR THE BROWN BUTTER SAUCE:

1 pound (4 sticks) unsalted butter

½ cup sundried tomatoes, chopped

¼ cup capers

Juice of 1½ lemons (about 4½ tablespoons)

Salt and freshly ground black pepper, to taste

Pickled onions, for garnish

Fresh fennel, for garnish

Grated Parmesan cheese, for serving

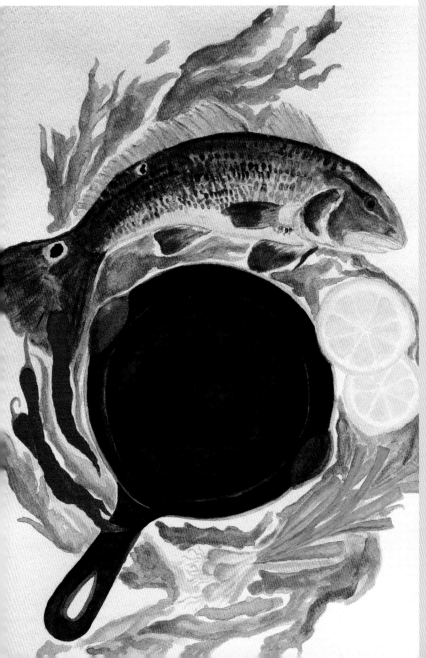

Baton Rouge ★

SERVES 1

FOR THE SAUCE:

1 peeled lemon, pith removed, with juice,

1 cup white wine

1 tablespoon Worcester-shire sauce

2 tablespoons veal or chicken stock

1 bay leaf

¼ cup small diced shallots

1½ sticks (12 tablespoons) unsalted butter, kept cold and cubed

Salt and freshly ground black pepper, to taste

FOR THE CRAB TOPPING:

2 tablespoons unsalted butter

1 ounce button mush-rooms, sliced

2 ounces Louisiana jumbo lump crabmeat, picked clean of shells

Salt and freshly ground black pepper, to taste

Splash of white wine

1 tablespoon thinly sliced green onions

SAUTÉED REDFISH FILET WITH LOUISIANA LUMP CRABMEAT
JUBAN'S RESTAURANT
JOEY DAIGLE, EXECUTIVE CHEF

Chef Daigle, a native of Plaquemine, Louisiana, is the new chef at Juban's, the award-winning restaurant that's been family owned and operated since 1983. True to Juban's elegant Creole menu, the classic meunière seafood sauce gets an extra kick from the addition of Worcestershire sauce. The restaurant uses sustainably farmed redfish in their preparation, but they suggest substituting black drum or other Gulf fish if redfish is not available. Although this recipe makes one serving, it can easily be doubled or quadrupled to serve more.

Make the sauce. Add the lemon, wine, Worcestershire sauce, stock, bay leaf, and shallots to small saucepan over medium heat. Reduce this mixture by two-thirds; it still should be a bit liquid. Turn off the fire, start adding the butter, and stir to combine. Strain through a fine-mesh sieve and season with salt and pepper. Keep hot.

Make the crab topping. Heat the butter in small skillet. Add the mushrooms and cook on high heat until they start to brown a bit. Add the crabmeat, toss, and season with salt and pepper. Add the white wine and green onions, toss, and keep hot.

Make the fish. Check the fish and remove any pin bones or scales; pat dry. In a shallow bowl, beat together the egg and milk. In another shallow dish, season the flour with salt and pepper. Heat the butter in a medium-sized oven-safe pan over medium-high heat. Dip the filet into the egg wash and then into the seasoned flour for a dusting. Place into the hot butter and cook for 2 minutes on each side, or until golden brown. Depending on the thickness of the fish filet, it should be done and ready to plate. Check with a sharp knife. If not cooked through, finish it in a 350°F oven. Lay the fish filet on the plate and top with the crab. Spoon the sauce over the top.

FOR THE REDFISH:

1 (7- to 8-ounce) Louisiana redfish filet, or other local fish

1 egg

¼ cup milk

¼ cup flour, for dusting

Salt and freshly ground pepper, to taste

2 to 3 tablespoons butter or vegetable oil

EMILY FOREMAN, *I'LL SLEEP TOMORROW*, PENCIL AND GRAPHITE

New Orleans ★

1 cup all-purpose flour

4 (6- to 7-ounce) Louisiana red snapper portions, scaled and scored

Salt and freshly ground pepper, to taste

2 tablespoons plus ½ cup (1 stick) salted butter, cut into ½-inch chunks, divided

2 tablespoons canola or olive oil

16 large chanterelle or shiitake mushroom caps

3 tablespoons chopped fresh pea shoots

½ pound fresh Louisiana jumbo lump crab, picked

2 ounces country or tasso ham, julienned

Whole pea shoots, for garnish

SAUTÉED LOUISIANA RED SNAPPER WITH CHANTERELLES
GW FINS
TENNEY FLYNN, CHEF/CO-OWNER

This restaurant, located in the heart of the French Quarter, features the finest seafood from around the world, but this recipe shows Chef Flynn's mastery of local fare.

Preheat two medium-sized sauté pans. Place the flour in a pie tin or dinner plate. Season both sides of the snapper with salt and black pepper and dredge into the flour. Place 1 tablespoon each of butter and oil into one of the preheated sauté pans. Remove the fish from the flour and shake off the excess. Place the filets skin-side down in the hot fat and cook on medium to high heat for about 4 minutes. Turn and continue cooking for another 2 minutes or so more.

Put 1 tablespoon each of the butter and oil in the other hot pan and add the mushroom caps. Cover and cook for 2 to 3 minutes, stirring occasionally.

Pour ¼ cup water in a thick coffee mug and microwave on high until boiling. Add the remaining ½ cup cut-up butter and blend with an immersion blender until creamy and emulsified. Add the pea shoots and continue blending until smooth. Reserve and keep warm.

Add the picked crabmeat and the julienned ham to the cooked shiitakes. Toss to heat.

To serve, divide the mushroom, ham, and crabmeat mixture equally in the center of four warmed plates. Pour 2 tablespoons of the pea shoot–butter sauce around the mushrooms, top with the fish filets and garnish with pea shoots. Serve immediately.

SNAPPER BROOKS
ERNEST'S ORLEANS RESTAURANT, ERNEST PALMISANO, JR., OWNER/CHEF

This dish is named for Mr. Leon Brooks, father of Kix Brooks (of Brooks and Dunn), country music legend and Shreveport native son.

Preheat the oven to 350°F.

Cover the bottom of a square baking pan with a little of the olive oil and set aside. In a separate dish, rub the snapper fillets with a little more olive oil, 1 teaspoon of the Worcestershire, and 1½ teaspoons of Ernest's Special Spice, if using. Roll the filets in 1½ cups of the breadcrumbs, enough to help seal the seasoning on the fish.

In another shallow dish, rub the oysters with a little more olive oil, and the remaining 1 teaspoon of the Worcestershire and 1½ teaspoons of Ernest's Special Spice. Roll the oysters in the remaining 1½ cups of the breadcrumbs.

Place the fillets in the prepared square baking pan and add the white wine. Place 6 oysters on top of each fillet. Bake for 20 minutes.

Note: Ernest's Special Spice is a Mediterranean-Creole blend that is the restaurant's house seasoning. It can be ordered by calling or emailing the restaurant.

Shreveport

SERVES 2

¾ cup olive oil, divided

2 (8-ounce) center-cut Louisiana red snapper fillets

2 teaspoons Lea & Perrins Worcestershire sauce, divided

3 teaspoons Ernest's Special Spice, divided (optional, see Note)

3 cups Italian breadcrumbs, divided

12 raw unwashed Louisiana Gulf oysters

¾ cup white wine

New Orleans ★

12 mirlitons

2 large onions

4 bell peppers (green, red, or yellow)

1 bunch celery

1 tablespoon minced or granulated garlic

½ cup (1 stick) butter

1½ pounds smoked ham

2 to 3 pounds peeled Louisiana shrimp, chopped

½ cup Italian breadcrumbs

½ cup plain breadcrumbs, plus more for topping

1 teaspoon salt (see Note)

½ teaspoon freshly ground black pepper

LOUISIANA SHRIMP-STUFFED MIRLITON
JACK DEMPSEY'S RESTAURANT
SAMMY BAIAMONTE, CHEF

This old-school restaurant, housed in a small white building in the Bywater neighborhood along the Mississippi River levee, isn't named for the famous fighter, but rather a boisterous New Orleans police reporter for the States-Item. First established by a pair of policemen who knew Dempsey well, the restaurant was purchased by Andrew and Diane Marino in 1980. Today, their son, Chef Baiamonte, serves an array of fried seafood platters and Po' Boys, along with family recipes like their famous macaroni and cheese and this stuffed mirliton. More commonly known as chayote to the rest of the country, the mirliton is a favorite food of southern Louisiana.

Cut the mirlitons in half and steam or parboil in a large pot for 30 to 45 minutes. Poke with a fork; if the meat is tender, take them out of the pot. Removed the seed from each and discard. Delicately hollow the mirliton by scraping the meat out. Don't scrape too close, you want the shell to have body to it for stuffing later. Set the meat aside and turn the shells upside-down to drain.

Preheat the oven to 300°F.

Chop the onions, bell peppers, and celery. Melt the butter in a Dutch oven and sauté the vegetables. While that is sautéing, cube the ham into small bite-sized pieces.

When the vegetables are translucent, add the ham and shrimp to the mixture. Add the salt, pepper, and garlic. When the shrimp are cooked (when they turn white), it is time to add the meat from the mirliton. Let the mixture simmer on a medium to low heat to blend the flavors for about 5 minutes.

Next, fold in the breadcrumbs. Because mirlitons are a watery vegetable, you may add more or less breadcrumbs than the recipe calls for to reach the desired consistency. You may also want to add more salt (see Note) and pepper to taste. Cook for 5 minutes more.

Place the mirliton shells in a casserole dish and stuff with the filling. Sprinkle a little more breadcrumbs on top and bake, covered, for 20 to 30 minutes.

Note: Because the ham and Italian breadcrumbs contain salt, you may want to add salt sparingly.

JACKLYN MARR, *PRODUCE OF LOUISIANA LIFE,* **WATERCOLOR**

ROY'S SEAFOOD FETTUCCINE
CAJUN LANDING
ROY ABSHIRE, CHEF

SERVES 6 TO 8

4 tablespoons butter

1½ tablespoon flour

1 quart heavy whipping cream

½ teaspoon white pepper

2 teaspoons granulated garlic

2 teaspoons onion powder

1 tablespoon Paul Prudhomme's Blackened Redfish Magic seasoning

1 tablespoon chicken base (see Note)

8 slices (6 ounces) Swiss-American cheese

½ cup grated Parmesan cheese

1½ cups sliced mushrooms

2 bunches green onions, thinly sliced

4 pounds cooked Louisiana seafood (shrimp and crawfish)

2 (12-ounce) packages fettuccine, cooked according to package directions

Cajun Landing is popular with locals and travellers alike, introducing many to traditional Louisiana seafood. The restaurant features a homey atmosphere and an excellent oyster bar.

Melt the butter in a medium-sized saucepan; when foaming, whisk in the flour and let cook for 1 minute. Pour in the cream and stir to combine. Add the white pepper, garlic onion powder, Redfish Magic, and chicken base and stir to combine.

Add the Swiss-American and Parmesan cheeses and continue to stir until the cheese is melted and well combined. Add the mushrooms, green onions and seafood. When just heated through, pour over the cooked pasta and toss gently to combine.

Note: Chicken base is highly concentrated chicken stock. Look for it in paste, powder or cubed form in the supermarket aisle next to bouillon, or order online.

CRABMEAT YVONNE
GALATOIRE'S BISTRO
KELLEY MCCANN/EXECUTIVE CHEF

An elegant preparation of Louisiana crabmeat as served at both Galatoire's in New Orleans and Galatoire's Bistro in Baton Rouge as well.

Make the meuniére butter. In medium saucepan over medium heat, melt the butter, whisking constantly, for 8 to 10 minutes, until the sediment in the butter turns dark brown, almost (but not quite) to the point of burning, and the liquid is a deep golden color. Remove the pan from the heat and continue to whisk slowly, adding the lemon juice and vinegar to the browned butter. The sauce will froth until the acids have evaporated. When the frothing subsides, the sauce is complete.

In a large pot, submerge the artichokes in water, add the lemon juice, and boil for approximately 30 minutes until the stems are tender. Peel all of the exterior leaves from the artichokes hearts. Using a spoon or your thumb, remove and discard the chokes, leaving only the bottoms. Cut the bottoms into slices. Set aside.

In a large skillet over medium heat, heat the meuniére butter. Add the mushrooms, artichokes, and scallions and sauté. Gently fold in the crabmeat and continue to sauté until the crabmeat is heated through. Remove from the heat and plate. Garnish with the lemon quarters, if desired.

Baton Rouge ★

SERVES 6

1 pound salted butter

1 tablespoon fresh lemon juice

1 tablespoon red wine vinegar

6 fresh artichokes

Juice of 1 lemon (about 3 tablespoons)

1 pound button mushrooms, sliced

1 bunch of scallions, chopped

1 pound jumbo Louisiana lump crabmeat, cleaned

Lemon quarters, for garnish (optional)

Thibodaux
★

SERVES 4

FOR THE CRABS:

1 cup (2 sticks) unsalted butter, divided

12 ounces sliced mushrooms

½ cup brandy

½ cup Lafourche Sauce

2½ cups heavy cream (40% fat content)

½ cup chopped spring onions (green part only)

4 ounces Louisiana jumbo lump crabmeat

Salt and pepper to taste

24 ounces angel hair pasta, cooked according to package directions

3 tablespoons dry Italian seasoning

4 tablespoons chopped parsley, divided

4 jumbo Louisiana soft shell crabs, fried in seasoned corn flour (see Note)

SOFT SHELL CRABS LAFOURCHE
FLANAGAN'S CREATIVE FOOD AND DRINK
RANDY BARRIOS, CHIEF EXECUTIVE CHEF

Thibodaux is the parish seat of Lafourche Parish, and it gives its name to this dish's mushroom cream sauce, a specialty of the house at Flanagan's. In addition to soft shell crabs in season, Chef Barrios also serves this dish with jumbo fried shrimp or fried Louisiana Gulf oysters. Fry the soft shell crabs just before serving.

Melt 2 tablespoons of the butter in a large sauté pan. Add the mushrooms and sauté until tender. Deglaze the pan with the brandy. Add the Lafourche sauce and the heavy cream and reduce by half, until the sauce coats the back of a spoon.

Add the green onions and jumbo lump crabmeat and simmer for 2 minutes. (Try not to break up the beautiful Louisiana crabmeat.) Salt and pepper to taste. Keep the sauce warm while you prepare the pasta.

In another sauté pan, melt the remaining butter; add the cooked pasta and toss to coat with the Italian seasoning and 2 tablespoons of the parsley. Salt and pepper to taste.

To serve, divide the pasta onto 4 plates, top each with a fried soft shell crab, and pour the Lafourche sauce over both. Sprinkle with the remaining chopped parsley.

Note: To fry soft shell crabs, heat four cups of vegetable oil to 365°F in a deep fryer or heavy-bottomed deep pan. Clean the crabs and pat dry. In a bowl, whisk together 1 egg and ½ cup milk. In another bowl, mix together 1 cup corn flour and salt and pepper to taste (substitute cayenne pepper, if you like). Coat the crabs in the seasoned flour, then in the egg wash, then in the seasoned flour again. Shake off any excess and carefully drop the crabs into the hot oil. Cook until golden brown, 1 to 2 minutes, then flip and cook until golden brown on the other side. Drain on paper towels.

LAFOURCHE SAUCE

Melt the margarine in a large sauté pan. Add the mushrooms, Worcestershire sauce, hot sauce, seafood base, minced garlic, and lemon juice to the pan and stir to combine. Add the white wine and reduce until most of the liquid is evaporated. Add the heavy cream and spring onions. Cook until reduced by half and the sauce coats the back of a spoon. Fold in the unsalted butter and salt and pepper to taste. Keep the sauce warm until ready to use.

Note: Seafood base is highly concentrated seafood stock. Look for it in paste, powder or cubed form in the supermarket aisle next to bouillon, or order online.

FOR THE LAFOURCHE SAUCE:

2 teaspoons margarine

10 thin slices of mushroom

2 teaspoons Lee & Perrins Worcestershire sauce

2 teaspoons Louisiana hot sauce

Pinch of seafood base (see Note)

Pinch of minced garlic

2 teaspoons lemon juice

½ cup white wine (don't use it if you wouldn't drink it!)

2 cups heavy cream (40% fat content)

4 teaspoons unsalted butter

¼ cup chopped spring onions (green part only)

Salt and freshly ground black pepper to taste

Baton Rouge

SERVES 6

1 cup finely chopped onion

½ cup finely chopped celery

¼ pound margarine or butter

½ cup all-purpose flour

1 (13-ounce) can evaporated milk

2½ cups grated American cheese, divided

2 egg yolks

1 teaspoon salt

½ teaspoon cayenne pepper

¼ teaspoon freshly ground black pepper

1 pound Louisiana white crabmeat

CRABMEAT AU GRATIN
DON'S SEAFOOD
BOO MOORE AND DUKE LANDRY, CO-OWNERS

Don's Crabmeat au Gratin is a recipe that was developed by several members of the Landry family. Over a period of five or six years, it was refined and perfected to become one of the Don's Restaurants (established 1934) most popular entrées. This delicious combination of lump crabmeat and cheese may also be served as a topping for crackers or for several broiled fish entrées. Although relatively simple to prepare, it packs a powerful taste punch.

Preheat the oven to 375°F.

Sauté the onions and celery in margarine until the onions are wilted. Add the flour and blend well. Gradually pour in the evaporated milk and add ½ cup of the grated cheese, stirring constantly. Add the egg yolks, salt, cayenne and black pepper; cook for 5 minutes. Put the crabmeat in a mixing bowl and pour the sauce over the crabmeat. Blend well and then transfer into a lightly greased, 8 x 10-inch casserole and sprinkle with the remaining grated cheese. Bake for 10 to 15 minutes, or until golden brown.

ALLISON STRAHAN, *C'EST LA VIE*, MIXED MEDIA

New Orleans ★

SERVES 4

2 pounds jumbo (21/25) Louisiana shrimp, shell-on

2 tablespoons Emeril's Original Essence, divided

½ teaspoon freshly ground black pepper, divided

2 tablespoons olive oil, divided

¼ cup chopped onions

2 tablespoons minced garlic

3 bay leaves

3 lemons, peeled and sectioned

½ cup Worcestershire sauce

¼ dry white wine

¼ teaspoon salt

2 cups heavy cream

2 tablespoons butter

Chopped chives, for garnish

EMERIL'S NEW ORLEANS BARBECUED SHRIMP WITH PETITE ROSEMARY BISCUITS

EMERIL'S NEW ORLEANS
EMERIL LAGASSE, OWNER/CHEF

Chef Lagasse opened his flagship New Orleans restaurant in 1990. Housed in a renovated pharmacy warehouse in the city's Warehouse District, the rustic yet sophisticated atmosphere highlights the chef's signature "New New Orleans" cuisine, featuring the best of local and seasonal ingredients. This recipe is adapted from New New Orleans Cooking, *by Emeril Lagasse and Jessie Tirsch, published by William Morrow (1993), courtesy Martha Stewart Living Omnimedia, Inc.*

Peel and devein the shrimp, leaving only their tails attached. Reserve the shells separately.

Sprinkle the shrimp with 1 tablespoon of the Essence and ¼ teaspoon of the pepper. Toss to coat the shrimp well and refrigerate the shrimp until you have made the sauce and the biscuits.

Make the sauce. Heat 1 tablespoon of the oil in a large pot over high heat. When the oil is hot, add the onions and garlic and sauté for 1 minute. Add the reserved shrimp shells, the remaining Essence, the bay leaves, lemons, 2 cups water, the Worcestershire, wine, salt, and the remaining ¼ teaspoon black pepper. Stir well and bring to a boil. Reduce the heat and simmer for 30 minutes. Remove from the heat, allow to cool for about 15 minutes, and strain into a small saucepan. There should be about 1½ cups. Place over high heat, bring to a boil, and cook until thick, syrupy, and dark brown, about 15 minutes longer. You should have 4 to 5 tablespoons of barbecue sauce base.

Make the biscuits according to directions and set aside to keep warm until ready to serve.

Heat the remaining 1 tablespoon of oil in a large skillet over high heat. When the oil is hot, add the shrimp and quickly sauté them, occasionally shaking the skillet, until almost cooked through, about 2 minutes. Add the cream and all of the barbecue sauce base. Stir and simmer for 3 minutes. Remove the shrimp to a warm platter. Cook the sauce until it is thick enough to coat the back of a spoon, 4 to 5 minutes longer. Whisk the butter into the sauce. Remove from the heat.

Arrange the shrimp in the center of four large dinner plates and spoon the sauce over the shrimp and around the plate. Arrange the biscuits around the shrimp. Garnish with chopped chives.

PETITE ROSEMARY BISCUITS
Preheat the oven to 400°F.

Sift the flour, baking powder, baking soda, and salt into a large mixing bowl.

Add the butter and, using your fingers or a pastry blender, work the butter into the flour until the mixture resembles coarse crumbs. Add ½ cup of the buttermilk, a little at a time, and using your hands, work it into the dry ingredients just enough to make a dough come together. If it seems dry, you can add up to 2 tablespoons more; this will depend on the humidity and the type of flour that you use. Be careful not to overwork or over-handle the dough, or the biscuits will be tough.

Transfer the dough to a lightly floured surface and pat into a thickness of about ½-inch. Using a 1-inch round cookie cutter, cut out 12 biscuits. Place the biscuits on a baking sheet and bake until golden on top and lightly browned on the bottom, 10 to 12 minutes. Serve warm.

FOR THE PETITE ROSE-MARY BISCUITS:

MAKES 12 MINI-BISCUITS

1 cup all-purpose flour

1 teaspoon baking powder

⅛ teaspoon baking soda

½ teaspoon salt

3 tablespoons cold unsalted butter, cut into cubes

½ cup plus 2 tablespoons buttermilk, divided

1 tablespoon minced fresh rosemary

New Orleans ★

SERVES 6

FOR THE HERRADURA MIX:

½ to ¾ cup sun-dried tomatoes, cut in strips

1 cup Chardonney

1 cup (2 sticks) butter

2 whole yellow onions, ¼-inch dice cut

2 teaspoons Chef Paul Prudhomme's Vegetable Magic

¼ teaspoon cayenne pepper

2.5 ounces Herradura tequila

1 quart chicken broth

3 pounds extra-large (21/30) Louisiana shrimp, peeled and deveined, tails left on

1 recipe Herradura mix

6 tablespoons pine nuts

4 to 6 teaspoons minced garlic

¼ cup ¼-inch chopped green onions

15 to 20 basil leaves

1½ sticks butter

1 quart fresh tomatoes, diced (about 3 pounds)

HERRADURA SHRIMP
DRAGO'S SEAFOOD RESTAURANT
TOMMY CVITANOVICH, CO-OWNER/CHEF

Chef Cvitanovich's parents, Drago and Klara, are still daily fixtures at the restaurant they opened in 1969 and were inducted into the Louisiana Restaurant Association's Hall of Fame in 2013. Famous for their charbroiled oysters, the menu features a wide range of seafood, as proved by this tequila-marinated shrimp preparation. The chef suggests serving with grilled, marinated (in olive oil and red wine vinegar) Portobello mushrooms, or over angel hair pasta.

Make the Herradura mix. Marinate the sun-dried tomato strips in Chardonnay until rehydrated, 1 to 2 hours.

In a heavy saucepan, melt the butter on medium heat. Add the onions and cook until caramelized. Add the marinated tomatoes and heat thoroughly. Add the Vegetable Magic and cayenne and mix well. Deglaze the pan with the tequila and carefully flame to burn off the alcohol. Allow to cool. You can store in the refrigerator up to 3 days.

Make the shrimp. Add the chicken broth to a large sauté pan. Add the shrimp and sauté for 1 to 2 minutes, then add the Herradura mix, pine nuts, garlic, green onions, basil leaves, butter, and tomatoes. Continue to cook until the liquid is reduced by a quarter and serve.

GRILLED TUNA WITH OLIVE SALAD
PÊCHE SEAFOOD GRILL
DONALD LINK, CO-OWNER/CHEF

New Orleans

Located in a former carriage house in the Warehouse District of New Orleans, Pêche is James Beard Award–winning chef Donald Link's temple of Gulf seafood, cooked on an open-fire hearth in full view of the dining room. Chef Link prefers to have the tuna portions cut into long rectangles instead of steaks, as it makes it easier to grill them evenly.

Combine the olives, spring onion, red wine vinegar, sherry vinegar, oil, garlic, parsley, and salt and pepper and mix well. Set aside.

Dry the fish with a paper towel and very lightly coat it with regular olive oil. Season the tuna liberally with kosher salt and pepper. Allow the fish to rest for 10 to 15 minutes at room temperature. This will allow the seasoning to really adhere and allow the interior to come up to room temp. I like my tuna served rare but do not enjoy having it ice cold in the center and well done on the exterior.

Build a bed of coals at medium-high heat. This can be tested by holding your hand over the coals for about three seconds before it is to hot and must be pulled away. Lightly oil the fish and the grill grates. Place the fish on the grill and leave it alone for 3 minutes. Do not cover the grill. Using a thin spatula work the fish gently off of the grates by gently lifting the edge and sliding under. Flip the fish onto the second side and cook for 2 to 3 minutes more. Flip it again and cook the third side for 2 minutes. Repeat for the fourth side but only cook for 1 to 2 minutes. Gently press on the fish to test for doneness. The exterior should be firm and not yield to pressure but the interior should be soft and give easily when gently pressed.

Transfer the fish to a cutting board and slice on a bias across the grain. Transfer the sliced tuna to a plate, spoon a generous amount of the olive salad over the fish and season with a good finishing salt.

SERVES 1

FOR THE OLIVE SALAD:

1 cup mixed pitted olives

1 small spring onion, julienned

3 tablespoons red wine vinegar

1 tablespoon sherry vinegar

6 tablespoon extra virgin olive oil

1 tablespoon chopped garlic

¼ cup picked parsley

Salt and pepper

1 (6- to 8-ounce) portion fresh tuna, cut from the center part of the loin

Olive oil

Kosher salt and pepper

Sea salt, for serving

Baton Rouge
★

SERVES 1

½ cup olive oil

½ cup Chipotle Salsa

½ pound large (31/35) Louisiana shrimp, peeled and deveined, tail left on

1 cup julienned yellow squash

1 cup julienned zucchini

1 cup julienned portobello mushrooms

½ cup white wine (drink the rest!)

1 cup of cooked or steamed brown rice or fresh baby spinach, for serving

Sautéed onions, for serving

Queso blanco, for serving

SHRIMP MEXICAN STIR FRY
MESTIZO RESTAURANT
JIM URDIALES, CHEF/OWNER

The word mestizo *means "of mixed blood" in Spanish and refers to owner Jim Urdiales's Mexican and Louisiana-French heritage. This third-generation restaurateur has been serving great Mexican cuisine to the city of Baton Rouge for ten years. This dish has been offered on the menu since 2008 and fast become a hit. It is the perfect dish for those health-conscious diners who want to cut back on calories. This dish serves one person as an entrée, but is easily doubled or quadrupled.*

Heat the olive oil in a large sauté pan and quickly add the Chipotle Salsa. Add the shrimp and sauté for about 1 minute. Add the squash, zucchini, and portobellos and stir continuously. (I prefer my veggies al dente for more nutritional value.) Add the white wine to the pan toward the end for steam to fully cook the vegetables. Serve over a bed of brown rice or fresh baby spinach and top with sautéed onions for more flavor. I also add queso blanco on the side for more flavor.

CAROLINE DELAHOUSSAY, *MAW MAW'S SHRIMP GUMBO, OIL AND ACRYLIC*

CHIPOTLE SALSA

Chef Urdiales suggests keeping any extra salsa in the refrigerator to add a little hint of flavor to many dishes.

Place the chipotle peppers, tomatoes, garlic, cilantro, red onion, and jalapeño in a blender with 1 cup of water. Add salt and pepper to taste. Blend until smooth.

FOR THE CHIPOTLE SALSA:

MAKES 3½ TO 4 CUPS

2 individual canned chipotle peppers in adobo sauce (I prefer the Embasa brand, found in the Hispanic foods aisle of the supermarket)

2 cups canned tomatoes

3 fresh garlic cloves

1 bunch cilantro leaves

1 large red onion, sliced

1 jalapeño or Serrano pepper for more heat

Salt and freshly ground black pepper, to taste

New Orleans ★

SERVES 4

FOR THE SHRIMP:

8 strips applewood-smoked bacon, cut crosswise into thirds

20 colossal (U-10) Louisiana shrimp (about 1¾ pounds), peeled and deveined, leaving tail intact

4 large wooden skewers, soaked in water for 10 minutes

Kosher salt and freshly ground black pepper, to taste

2 tablespoons vegetable oil

2 tablespoons apple cider vinegar

3½ teaspoons firmly packed dark brown sugar

2½ cups dark chicken stock (see Note)

2½ tablespoons pepper jelly

1 tablespoon cold unsalted butter

3 cups Mr. B's Stone-Ground Grits

2 tablespoons minced fresh chives

SHRIMP WITH RED-EYE GRAVY AND GRITS
MR. B'S BISTRO
MICHELLE McRANEY, EXECUTIVE CHEF

Owned and managed by Cindy Brennan, of the legendary Brennan family, this elegant French Quarter bistro offers authentic Creole food made from seasonal ingredients. According to Chef McRaney, "Every time this dish appears on the menu, our customers demand the recipe. We've spiced up this low-country classic, giving it heat and sweetness from pepper jelly and smokiness from bacon. Pepper jelly (made from bell peppers and jalapeños) is an indispensable ingredient to have on hand. You can slather it on pork tenderloin before you cook it, add a teaspoon to vinaigrette, or serve it alongside lamb chops." Pepper jelly can be found at specialty food stores and some supermarkets.

Wrap 1 piece bacon around center of each shrimp (reserve leftover bacon) and line up on a work surface. Skewer 5 wrapped shrimp onto each skewer, leaving a little space in between each shrimp. Season shrimp with salt and pepper.

Heat a large skillet over high heat. Add 1 tablespoon of the oil and heat until almost smoking. Add 2 skewers and cook 2 minutes each side, or until the bacon gets crisp, and transfer to a platter. Cook the remaining skewers in the same manner.

To the same skillet, add the vinegar and brown sugar and cook about 1 minute, or until reduced by half. Add the chicken stock and cook over high heat until reduced by half. Add the pepper jelly and cook 1 minute, or until jelly is dissolved. Remove the skillet from heat and add the butter, stirring, until just melted. Adjust seasoning with salt and pepper.

In a small skillet cook the leftover bacon until crisp. Cool and crumble.

To serve, mound the grits on the plates. Remove shrimp from skewers and arrange around grits. Drizzle the sauce over the grits and garnish with the extra bacon and the chives.

Note: Dark chicken stock is made with bones that have first been roasted, which give it a darker color and richer flavor than traditional stock.

MR. B'S STONE-GROUND GRITS

Stone-ground grits are night and day from instant grits. They have more of the kernel of the corn and their texture when cooked is heartier. Do not use instant grits here, they won't work.

In a medium saucepan bring the cream and the milk to a simmer over moderately low heat. Whisk in the grits and cook, stirring often, for 25 minutes. Stir in the cheese and season with salt and pepper.

FOR THE GRITS:

SERVES 4

2 cups heavy cream

2 cups whole milk

1 cup stone-ground grits

⅓ cup mascarpone cheese

Kosher salt and freshly ground black pepper, to taste

TYE ANDERSON, *MUDDY WATERS,* **PENCIL AND GRAPHITE (FIFTH PLACE JUNIOR)**

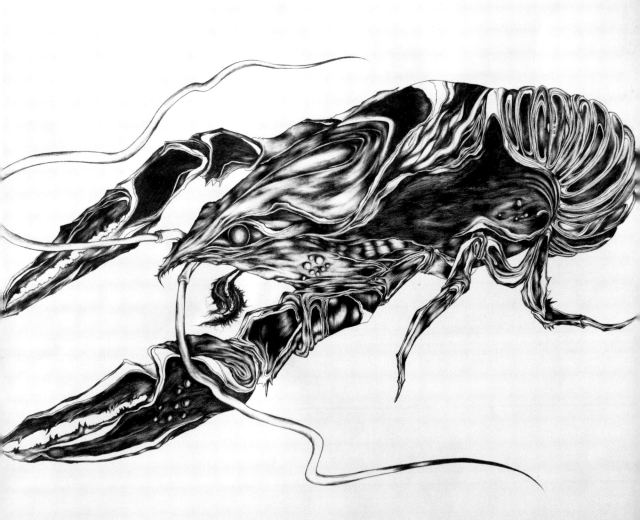

New Orleans

SERVES 6 (½ SLAB OF RIBS AND 3 SHRIMP PER PERSON)

FOR THE RIBS AND BRINE:

3 (2- to 3-pound) slabs St. Louis–style pork ribs

1 pound brown sugar

1 pound salt

FOR THE SPICY LEMON-GRASS MARINADE:

2 stalks lemongrass, peeled and bruised, cut into 2-inch lengths

2 stalks lemongrass, shredded

1 large yellow onion, chopped

2 cloves garlic, peeled

¼ cup cilantro, stems removed

½ cup plus 1 tablespoon brown sugar

½ cup plus 1 tablespoon white sugar

¼ cup fish sauce

¼ cup soy sauce

2 tablespoons rice vinegar

1 teaspoon chili-garlic paste

(Continued)

SPICY LEMONGRASS GRILLED SHRIMP WITH STRAWBERRY-GLAZED PORK RIBS
NOCCA CULINARY ARTS PROGRAM
SIERRA TORRES, NOCCA CULINARY ARTS STUDENT

Ninth grader Sierra Torres created the winning recipe in the 2013 Dish That Makes a Difference recipe contest for students in NOCCA's Culinary Arts Program. In this competition, pioneered by the Emeril Lagasse Foundation, three dishes from each student are judged by New Orleans chefs and restaurateurs. Versions of the winning dish appeared on restaurant menus across the city, with a portion of the proceeds donated to the NOCCA Institute to support Louisiana's next generation of culinary artists.

Brine the ribs. In a large container, combine 5 gallons of water with the brown sugar and salt. Add the ribs and let brine for at least 6 hours, or overnight.

Make the lemongrass marinade. Halve and separate the layers of 2 stalks of lemongrass and bruise with a mallet or the bottom of a knife handle; set aside. In a food processor, pulse the remaining lemongrass with the onion, garlic and cilantro. Combine the brown sugar, white sugar, fish sauce, soy sauce, rice vinegar, chili-garlic paste, chili paste, lemon zest and juice, sesame oil, vegetable oil, hot chili oil, and ¾ cup of water in a large mixing bowl and stir until sugar is dissolved. Add the bruised lemongrass and the onion-garlic mixture.

Remove the ribs from the brine and marinate overnight in the spicy lemongrass marinade, reserving about 1 cup to marinate the shrimp.

Make the strawberry glaze. Half the lemongrass and rough chop; add to a food processor with the strawberries, ginger, basil, onion, garlic, and cilantro. Pulse until roughly shredded and transfer to a medium-sized non-reactive saucepan. Add the fish sauce brown sugar, white sugar, soy sauce, rice vinegar, chili-garlic paste, chili paste, honey, molasses, lemon zest and juice, sesame oil, hot chili oil, and ¾ cup of water, and stir over medium-high heat; bring to a simmer and cook down for 15 to 20 minutes until the flavors are well developed. Strain the mixture through a fine-mesh sieve, return to the stove and bring the liquid to a boil. Wet cornstarch with cold water and add the slurry to liquid; return to a boil and cook until thickened.

Cook the ribs. Preheat the oven to 380°F. Cut slabs in half and wrap each half individually in plastic wrap, then tightly in foil. Cook in oven for about 2½ hours. Let cool for 15 minutes before unwrapping. Reheat the ribs on the grill, adding several layers of the strawberry glaze while grilling. Reserve the remaining strawberry glaze for serving.

(Continued on next page.)

MORGAN BARRANCO, *CHEF EXTRAORDINAIRE*, MIXED MEDIA

1 teaspoon chili paste

Zest of 1 large lemon (2 to 3 teaspoons)

Juice of 1 large lemon (about 3 tablespoons)

2 tablespoons sesame oil

¾ cup vegetable oil

1 teaspoon hot chili oil

FOR THE STRAWBERRY BBQ GLAZE:

2 stalks lemongrass

1 quart strawberries, hulled and quartered

2 tablespoons peeled and chopped ginger

3 tablespoons chopped basil leaves

1 large yellow onion, chopped

2 cloves garlic, chopped

¼ cup cilantro, stems removed

¼ cup fish sauce

½ cup plus 1 tablespoon brown sugar

½ cup plus 1 tablespoon white sugar

¾ cup soy sauce

2 tablespoons rice vinegar

1 teaspoon chili-garlic paste

1 teaspoon chili paste

2 ounces honey

2 ounces molasses

Zest of 1 large lemon (2 to 3 teaspoons)

(Continued)

Juice of 1 large lemon (about 3 tablespoons)

2 tablespoons sesame oil

1 teaspoon hot chili oil

2 tablespoons cornstarch

FOR THE SHRIMP:

18 (about ¾ pound) jumbo (11/15) Louisiana shrimp

Spicy Lemongrass Marinade

3 cups good-quality store-bought kimchi, for serving

½ pound Louisiana lump crabmeat, for serving

½ pint strawberries, sliced, for serving

6 good-quality store-bought Chinese steamed buns, for serving

Make the shrimp. Peel and clean the shrimp; marinate for 1 hour in the remaining spicy lemongrass marinade. Place shrimp on grill and cook for 2 minutes. Flip and cook for 2 minutes more, until pink.

To serve. After grilling, cut the slab along the bones into individual ribs. Stack 3 to 4 ribs in the center of each plate and arrange 3 grilled shrimp around the ribs. Toss the kimchi with the fresh crab and sliced strawberries and place on top of the ribs; drizzle the plates with the remaining strawberry glaze. Serve with Chinese steamed buns.

CAROLINE BLANCHET, *CRAWFISH TIME*, OIL AND ACRYLIC

LOUISIANA CRAWFISH ÉTOUFFÉE
THE SHREVEPORT CLUB
KEITH LENARD, EXECUTIVE CHEF

Like gumbo, étouffée is a classic dish of both Cajun and Creole cuisine. And, like gumbo, you'll find that every southern Louisiana cook has his or her own recipe for the dish. Here is crawfish étouffée as it is served at The Shreveport Club.

In a tall soup pot, melt the butter and add the celery, bell pepper, and onions. Sweat the vegetables until they are completely translucent, but do not let them caramelize.

Add 2 quarts of water to the pot, along with the bay leaves, Cajun seasoning, garlic powder, and salt. Bring to a boil.

Thicken with Clearjel or cornstarch until the liquid coats the back of a spoon. Let it boil slowly for 15 to 20 minutes, but do not let the liquid reduce too much.

When ready to serve, add the crawfish tails along with the fat and all of the liquid in the bag. Let it boil no more than 3 minutes. Stir with a spoon to make sure all the submerged crawfish tails are incorporated. Serve over boiled white rice.

Note: Clearjel is a cornstarch derivative used for thickening. Look for it in the baking aisle, or order online.

Shreveport

SERVES 12

½ cup (1 stick) butter

1 pound celery, diced small

1 pound green bell pepper, diced small

1 pound white onions, diced small

2 bay leaves

Tony Chachere's Cajun Seasoning (or your favorite Cajun seasoning), to taste

¼ cup garlic powder

Salt, to taste

Clearjel (see Note) or cornstarch, for thickening

3 pounds Louisiana crawfish tails, with fat

Cook white rice, for serving

Monroe

SERVES 4

1 (17¼-ounce) package puff pastry (2 sheets thawed)

½ pound peeled Louisiana crawfish tails

1 teaspoon Creole seasoning

1 teaspoon olive oil

1 tablespoon minced garlic

1 tablespoon minced shallot

1½ tablespoons minced red onion

1 cup heavy cream

1½ teaspoons hot sauce

1½ teaspoons Worcestershire sauce

¼ teaspoon salt

Pinch of white pepper

2 tablespoon finely chopped green onion

1 tablespoon unsalted butter

8 whole chives for garnish

LOUISIANA CRAWFISH IN BACCO CREAM SAUCE
BACCO ITALIAN GRILLE
CHAD MATRANA, CHEF

This elegant treatment of crawfish tails sets the seafood in a puff pastry shell, served with a nicely spiced cream sauce.

Preheat the oven to 400°F. Line a baking sheet with parchment paper and set aside.

Roll out the pastry on a lightly floured surface to a 13x12-inch rectangle. Trim the pastry to a 10-inch square and cut into quarters to make four 5-inch squares.

Fold 1 square diagonally in half to form a triangle and place on your work surface with the folded side closest to you.

Starting ½-inch from the bottom corners of the triangle, cut a ½-inch border along the top two sides, leaving the bottom corners in tact. Unfold the triangle and using your fingers, brush the ½-inch strips with water. Fold the right underneath the left strip and the left strip over the right strip, wet sides down, and press firmly into place and make a diamond shape with raised borders. Repeat the process with the remaining squares. Place the pastries on the prepared baking sheet and bake until set and light golden brown, 18 to 20 minutes. Transfer pastries to a wire rack when done.

Season the crawfish with the Creole seasoning.

Heat the oil in a large sauté pan over medium heat. Add the garlic, shallot, and red onion cooking until translucent. Cook and stir for about 1 minute. Add the crawfish and cook, stirring for 1 minute. Add the cream, hot sauce, Worcestershire sauce, salt and pepper. Bring to a boil. Reduce the heat and simmer until the sauce is thick and the volume is reduced by half. Add the green onions and butter. Stir and remove from heat. Add seasoning to taste.

To serve, spoon about 1 tablespoon of the sauce into the center of four plates and arrange the pastries on top. Fill the pastries with the crawfish and the remaining sauce, garnish the top of each with 2 chives, and serve immediately.

ASHLEY ROTH, *PINCH ME*, OIL AND ACRYLIC

Baton Rouge ★

LOUISIANA CRAWFISH BOIL PASTA
RAISING CANE'S
TODD GRAVES, FOUNDER

SERVES 4

1 pound fresh pasta, shape of your choice

4 tablespoons salt

2 tablespoons olive oil

1 cup Strong Crawfish Stock

½ cup (1 stick) butter

2 tablespoons olive oil

½ cup chopped onions

½ cup diced andouille sausage

1 tablespoon minced garlic

1 cup corn (shelled from boiled cobs or frozen kernels)

1 cup diced potatoes

½ cup tomatoes, peeled, seeded, and diced

½ cup sliced mushrooms

½ cup sliced artichokes hearts

2 cups boiled and peeled Louisiana crawfish tails or 1 package crawfish tails

½ cup sliced green onions

¼ cup chopped Italian (flat-leaf) parsley

Sea salt and fresh ground black pepper, to taste

Although Raising Cane's has multiple locations across the state and beyond, this chain, known for its chicken fingers, maintains its home base in Baton Rouge. Todd Graves, the restaurant's founder, shares this recipe from his personal collection, saying, "Peter Sclafani, my friend (and executive chef and partner of Ruffino's restaurant) gave me this great pasta recipe made with leftovers from a crawfish boil to enjoy with my family. I tweaked his original recipe just a bit. If you are like me, you like a lot of different things to boil and pick up the flavor of the spices. Depending on the spice of your crawfish boil, using the leftovers from it may make for a very spicy dish, so if you like less spice you can choose fresh ingredients. Just double the cook time."

In a large pot, bring 1 gallon of water to a vigorous boil. Add the salt and olive oil to the water. Drop in the pasta while stirring. Cook until the pasta is al dente. Drain.

In a small saucepan, bring the crawfish stock to a boil. Cut the butter into pieces and pour the hot stock over it. Let it sit for 1 minute. Blend with an immersion blender. Set aside.

Heat the olive oil in a large sauté pan over medium high heat. Add the onion and andouille, sauté for 2 minutes. Add the garlic and cook 1 minute more. Stir in the corn, potatoes, tomatoes, mushrooms, artichoke hearts, and crawfish and cook for 1 minute. Reduce the heat to low and pour in the crawfish butter and cooked pasta. Garnish with green onions and parsley. Season to taste with salt and pepper. Divide into four bowls.

STRONG CRAWFISH STOCK

In a large stockpot, combine the crawfish shells, onion, celery, carrots, garlic, bay leaves, tomatoes, tomato paste, tarragon, peppercorns and coriander with 4 quarts of water. Make sure the shells are covered by the water. Place over medium high heat until it comes to a boil. Reduce the heat to a simmer and cook for 1½ hours. Skim any impurities while simmering. When finished simmering, strain and discard the solids. Return the stock to the stove and simmer until reduced by half.

REBECCA HODNETT, *MY LUZIANNE*, OIL AND ACRYLIC

FOR THE STRONG CRAWFISH STOCK:

3 pounds crawfish shells and heads (left over from a crawfish boil)

1 large onion, sliced

2 ribs celery, sliced

2 carrots, sliced

8 cloves garlic, smashed

2 bay leaves

2 tomatoes, chopped

2 tablespoons tomato paste

1 teaspoon tarragon

1 tablespoon black peppercorns

1 tablespoon coriander

Baton Rouge ★

4 ounces cream cheese

2 cups heavy cream

1 pound elbow pasta, shells, or mezze rigatoni

¼ cup green onions, sliced thin

2 pounds Louisiana crawfish tails

½ cup shredded fontina cheese

½ cup shredded Gruyère cheese

Sea salt and freshly ground black pepper, to taste

½ cup panko breadcrumbs

½ cup grated Parmigiano-Reggiano

1 tablespoon white truffle oil

1 teaspoon Creole seasoning

CRAWFISH MAC & CHEESE
RUFFINO'S
PETER SCLAFANI, CO-OWNER/EXECUTIVE CHEF

Chef Sclafani has gained culinary renown for his unique blend of southern Italian and French Creole cuisine. This third-generation chef is equally known for celebrating regional and seasonal ingredients. Here's his Italian-Creole take on an American classic.

Preheat the oven to 350°F.

In a mixing bowl, whisk together the cream cheese and heavy cream and blend until smooth.

Cook the pasta in plenty of boiling salted water until al dente. Drain well. Pour the hot pasta into the bowl with the cream cheese and cream. Add the green onions, crawfish, fontina, Gruyère, salt and pepper, and mix until well blended.

In a small mixing bowl, blend the panko, Parmigiano, truffle oil, and Creole seasoning.

Divide the paste into individual casseroles. Top with equal amounts of the breadcrumb mixture. Bake until hot and the topping is crisp, about 15 minutes.

ELAINA MANUEL, *PASS A GOOD TIME*, PENCIL AND GRAPHITE

CHAPTER FIVE
SIDE DISHES

DERRA LEONARD, *CAJUN INGREDIENTS*, OIL AND ACRYLIC

New Orleans ★

SERVES 8

8 Louisiana sweet potatoes

1 cup (2 sticks) butter, at room temperature

½ cup chopped pecans

¼ cup light brown sugar

2 tablespoons Steen's molasses (see Note, page 25)

BAKED SWEET POTATOES WITH PECAN BUTTER
DICKIE BRENNAN'S STEAKHOUSE
ALFRED SINGLETON, CHEF DE CUISINE

These dressed up baked sweet potatoes are the perfect accompaniment for steaks or pork tenderloin, especially during the holidays. Or, for a great light lunch or vegetarian dinner, pair them with a big tossed green salad.

Preheat the oven to 350°F. Place the sweet potatoes on a sheet pan and bake for 1 hour, or until soft to the touch. In a small bowl, mix together the butter, chopped pecans, light brown sugar, and molasses. Slice baked sweet potatoes lengthwise and top with about 2 tablespoons of the pecan butter.

KALLI PADGETT, *LOUISIANA JUICE*, OIL AND ACRYLIC (SECOND PLACE JUNIOR)

SERVES 6

5 tablespoons plus
2 teaspoons Chef Paul
Prudhomme's Pork and
Veal Magic

2 teaspoons dry mustard

1½ teaspoons basil

1½ teaspoons thyme

7 large onions, divided

½ cup coarsely chopped
pecans

4 tablespoons unsalted
butter

½ cup chopped green
bell pepper

¼ cup chopped celery

½ pound ground lean pork

½ teaspoon minced garlic

¾ cup uncooked converted
rice

2 cups chopped fresh
mushrooms

2 cups pork or chicken
stock, divided

1 (12-ounce) can
evaporated milk

2 cups grated Monterey
Jack cheese

BAKED STUFFED ONIONS
K-PAUL'S LOUISIANA KITCHEN
PAUL PRUDHOMME, OWNER/CHEF

Almost everyone uses onion as seasoning, but in this recipe it's a vegetable on its own. With a delicious meat stuffing that enhances the delicate sweet flavor, it takes the spotlight as a beautiful dish in its own right.

Combine the Pork and Veal Magic, dry mustard, basil, and thyme in a small bowl and set aside. Reserve 2 tablespoons of this spice mixture.

Peel the onions, chop 1 (you should have 1¼ cups) and set aside. Cut a thin slice off the top of each of the remaining onions so they will stand without tipping. Turn each onion over and scoop out the insides with a melon baller, leaving a shell about ½-inch thick. Cut a very thin slice off each of the 4 sides of each onion to keep them from rolling in the skillet, so they will brown evenly.

Toast the pecans in a dry 10-inch skillet over medium heat, flipping and shaking or stirring them until they are lightly roasted, about 3 minutes. Remove the pecans from the skillet and set them aside.

Wipe the skillet clean, return it to high heat, and add the butter. When the butter sizzles, add the onion cups, laying them on their sides, and cook, turning occasionally, until they are browned on all sides, about 2 minutes. Remove the onion cups and set aside.

To the skillet add ¾ cup of the chopped onions, all the peppers and celery, and cook until they are browned, about 4 minutes. Add the pork and garlic and cook until browned, breaking up the meat with a spoon, about 3 minutes. Stir in 1 tablespoon of the seasoning mix and the remaining ½ cup chopped onions, and cook for 1 minute. Stir in the rice and the remaining 4 tablespoons plus 1 teaspoon seasoning mix and cook for 3 minutes. Add the mushrooms and cook for 1 minute, scraping as the mixture begins to stick to the bottom of the skillet. Stir in 1¼ cups of the stock and cook until it is reduced and the mixture forms a crust on the bottom of the skillet, about 8 minutes. Add the evaporated milk and pecans, and scrape the skillet. Bring to a rolling boil, cover, and remove from the heat. Let sit, covered, for 20 minutes.

Preheat the oven to 375°F. Sprinkle each onion cup all over with 1 teaspoon each of the reserved seasoning mix, rubbing the mixture inside and out. Place the onions, open ends up, in a baking pan just large enough to hold them. Fill them with the pork-rice mixture, heaping it up as much as possible, and sprinkle the grated cheese on top. Pour the remaining ¾ cup stock into the bottom of the pan, and bake for 20 minutes. Turn the oven up to 550°F and bake another 10 minutes, or until brown and bubbly on top. Serve with a little sauce from the pan spooned over each onion.

ALI MUNJY, *GENIUSNESS MEETS DELICIOUSNESS*, PENCIL AND GRAPHITE

Metairie ★

SERVES 4

FOR THE CRUST:

¾ cup brown sugar

¼ cup all-purpose flour

¾ cup chopped nuts, preferably pecans

¼ cup melted butter

FOR THE SWEET POTATO MIXTURE:

¾ cup sugar

¼ teaspoon salt

¼ teaspoon pure vanilla extract

2 cups cooked mashed sweet potatoes

1 egg, well beaten

4 tablespoons butter

SWEET POTATO CASSEROLE
RUTH'S CHRIS STEAK HOUSE
MICHAEL MILLER, GENERAL MANAGER

Chris Matulich founded the original Chris Steak House in 1927; the restaurant was located on Broad Street, near the New Orleans Fairgrounds Racetrack. Ruth Fertel purchased the restaurant in 1965, and for many years would only hire single mothers to make up her all-female wait staff. The building burned down in 1976, and with a new location a few blocks away came the new name: Ruth's Chris Steakhouse. Today, this national restaurant group has four locations in Louisiana, including New Orleans (inside Harrah's Hotel) and Metaire. During the Thanksgiving and Christmas holidays, the restaurant makes this popular sweet potato casserole available in family-sized quantities for take-out, so folks can enjoy it at home.

Preheat the oven to 350°F. In a mixing bowl, stir together the brown sugar, flour, nuts, and butter. Set aside.

In another mixing bowl, combine the sugar, salt, vanilla, sweet potatoes, egg, and butter. Mix until thoroughly combined.

Pour the sweet potato mixture into buttered baking dish, then sprinkle the crust mixture evenly over the top. Bake for 30 minutes; allow to set for at least 30 minutes before serving.

DIRTY RICE
SLAP YA MAMA
WALKER & SONS, OWNERS

Here's the Walker family recipe for this traditional Cajun dish. It gets its name from the chicken giblets, which make the rice look "dirty." This is an excellent side dish for baked or fried chicken; or add chicken or sausage to the rice and serve it as a main.

Heat the bacon fat in a large skillet. Add the shallots, celery, and chicken giblets and sauté until golden brown. Add the tomato paste, pepper sauce, rice, Cajun seasoning, and 4 cups of water. Bring to a rolling boil, then turn down the heat, cover, and simmer 25 to 30 minutes, stirring occasionally. Remove the lid and let stand for 5 to 10 minutes. Adjust seasoning to taste, fluff with fork, and serve.

Ville Platte

SERVES 4

2 tablespoons bacon fat

¾ cup chopped shallots

1 rib celery, finely chopped

Pinch of chopped fresh parsley

1 pound chicken giblets, finely chopped or ground

1 tablespoon tomato paste

½ teaspoon Slap Ya Mama Cajun Pepper Sauce

2 cups rice

Slap Ya Mama Cajun Seasoning, to taste

Ville Platte

SERVES 8

1 pound dried kidney beans

¼ cup olive oil

1 pound sausage, sliced

1 large onion, chopped

1 green bell pepper, chopped

2 tablespoons minced garlic

2 stalks celery, chopped

2 bay leaves

1 teaspoon thyme

¼ teaspoon sage

1 tablespoon parsley

1 tablespoon Slap Ya Mama Cajun Seasoning

1⅓ cups uncooked white rice

RED BEANS AND RICE
SLAP YA MAMA
WALKER & SONS, OWNERS

This Creole dish is so closely associated with New Orleans that native son Louis Armstrong would famously sign his letters "Red Beans and Ricely Yours." Red beans and rice are traditionally made on Monday (wash day) to incorporate the leftovers from Sunday dinner and cook unatttended in a single pot. This Slap Ya Mama version could be a meal in itself, but a pork chop would go nicely on the side. Note that the beans are soaked overnight.

Rinse the beans in cold water and then soak them overnight in a large pot of water.

In a skillet, heat the oil over medium heat then add the sausage, onion, bell pepper, garlic, and celery and cook for 3 to 4 minutes. Rinse the beans and transfer them into a pot with 6 cups of water. Stir the cooked sausage and vegetables into the beans. Add the bay leaves, thyme, sage, parsley, and Cajun seasoning. Bring to a boil, reduce heat to medium-low and let simmer for 2½ hours, or until the beans are cooked.

Meanwhile, prepare the rice. In a saucepan, cover the rice with 2½ cups water and bring to a boil. Reduce heat, cover and simmer for 20 minutes. Serve the beans over the rice.

POTATOES AU GRATIN
DICKIE BRENNAN'S STEAKHOUSE
ALFRED SINGLETON, CHEF DE CUISINE

These luxurious potatoes, made with three different cheeses, are the perfect complement to the prime steaks served at Dickie Brennan's.

Preheat the oven to 300°F.

Slice potatoes lengthwise about ¹/₁₆-inch thick. Mix together the Gruyère, mozzarella, and cheddar. Place a layer of potatoes in the bottom of baking pan, then top with a mixture of the shredded cheeses and add a pinch of salt and pepper. Repeat this process until pan is filled to about 1 inch from the top. Add heavy cream evenly to the pan and finish with 1 layer of mixed cheese on top.

Press the potatoes and cheese down in the pan just to compact a little. Cover with parchment paper and foil and bake for 1 hour on the top rack of the oven.

Remove the pan from the oven and reduce the heat to 200°F. Sprinkle breadcrumbs on top of the potatoes; re-cover and rotate the pan as you return it to the oven. Bake for another 20 to 30 minutes or until potatoes are fork tender and the breadcrumbs are golden brown.

New Orleans
★

SERVES 8 TO 10

10 large Idaho potatoes

1 pound shredded Gruyère cheese

1 pound shredded mozzarella cheese

1 pound shredded white cheddar cheese

1 quart heavy whipping cream

Salt and freshly ground black pepper, to taste

1 cup breadcrumbs

New Orleans ★

MAKES 1 QUART

½ yellow onion, chopped

3 pints fresh blueberries

4 tablespoons tomato puree

½ cup Steen's cane vinegar (see Note, page 25)

1 cup orange or other fruit blossom honey

1 cup brewed Community Coffee New Orleans Blend with Chicory

3 bananas, roasted (see Note)

1 tablespoon chili powder

½ teaspoon cayenne pepper

Salt and freshly ground black pepper, to taste

BLUEBERRY COFFEE BARBEQUE SAUCE
DICKIE BRENNAN'S PALACE CAFE
BRANDON MUETZEL, CHEF DE CUISINE

The Palace Café serves contemporary Creole cuisine in an upbeat atmosphere housed in the historic Werlein's Music Building at the edge of the French Quarter. Community Coffee is a family-owned company that began more than 90 years ago in Baton Rouge. Its coffee is a staple at restaurants and in homes across Louisiana; look for it in specialty coffee shops or order online. Pair this sauce with roasted duck, rotisserie chicken, or grilled pork tenderloin.

In a saucepan over medium heat, cook the onion and blueberries until onions are translucent. Add tomato puree and cook 5 minutes more. Add the cane vinegar, honey, brewed coffee, and roasted bananas. Bring to a simmer and stir in the chili powder, cayenne, and salt and pepper. When thickened enough to coat the back of a spoon (10 to 15 minutes), remove from heat and purée.

Note: To roast bananas, preheat the oven to 350°F. Place 3 whole, unpeeled bananas on a baking sheet and roast until the skin turns black, 15 to 20 minutes. Let cool. Take off skin and discard.

LOUISIANA PECAN AND DATE PESTO
DOMENICA RESTAURANT
JOHN BESH, CO-OWNER, ALON SHAYA, CO-OWNER/CHEF

New Orleans

Chefs Besh and Shaya opened this authentic, family-oriented Italian restaurant in the historic Roosevelt Hotel in 2008. This pesto typifies their love of local ingredients in season. Chef Shaya says, "This is a great winter pesto using sweet dates and fresh Louisiana pecans. I use Italian parsley here since its season is prime in the winter and its flavor stands up to the toasted pecans and aged balsamic in the recipe. This pesto is great for fall dishes that may include Louisiana wild game, duck or pork. I also like to eat it drizzled over some really good ricotta from Bellwether farms with grilled bread."

Mix together the pecans, parsley leaves, Parmigiano reggiano, pecan oil, and kosher salt in the bowl of a food processor. Lightly pulse all ingredients together until well combined, but not totally pureed. (It will come together pretty quickly.)

Remove from the food processor and place into a mixing bowl. Fold in the chopped dates and balsamic vinegar. Use within 1 day of making.

MAKES 2 CUPS

½ cup chopped Louisiana pecans

½ cup Italian (flat-leaf) parsley leaves, lightly packed with stems removed

¼ cup grated Parmigiano reggiano cheese

½ cup pecan or canola oil

1 teaspoon kosher salt

4 dates, seed removed, chopped fine

2 teaspoons good-quality balsamic vinegar

CHAPTER SIX
DESSERTS

DAVIN ROBERSON, *FAT TUESDAY*, OIL AND ACRYLIC

New Orleans ★

SERVES 4

**FOR THE SPICY
CANDIED WALNUTS:**

1 cup walnuts, toasted

1 cup confectioners sugar

1 tablespoon cinnamon

¼ teaspoon cayenne
pepper

3 tablespoons sugar

1 quart boiling water

1 quart peanut oil

¼ teaspoon nutmeg

½ teaspoon kosher salt

**FOR THE FRENCH
TOAST:**

2 eggs

1 cup half-and-half

1 French baguette loaf or
other French-style bread
loaf, sliced

½ cup (1 stick) unsalted
butter

1 teaspoon cinnamon

1 tablespoon sugar

¼ teaspoon nutmeg

BANANAS FOSTER FRENCH TOAST WITH SPICY CANDIED WALNUTS
RESTAURANT STANLEY
SCOTT BOSWELL, OWNER/EXECUTIVE CHEF

Breakfast and brunch are served all day at this palace of comfort food on historic Jackson Square. In addition to the "world famous" burger, the restaurant also features a soda fountain and house-made ice cream. Serve this for a special brunch or simply as a tribute to New Orleans' most famous dessert.

Make the candied walnuts. Place a wire rack on a baking sheet. Place the toasted nuts in a hand-held strainer and submerse in the boiling water for 30 seconds. Remove and blot dry on a clean kitchen towel. Toss in a bowl with the confectioners sugar. Heat the peanut oil in a deep-fryer or deep saucepan until almost smoking. Working with one half of the nuts at a time, put the nuts back in the strainer and lower into the hot oil for 5 seconds; remove and spill out onto the wire rack. Mix the cinnamon, nutmeg, cayenne, sugar, and salt together and dust over the hot walnuts. Let cool. Set the oil aside.

Prepare the French toast. Place a wire rack on a baking sheet. Mix the eggs and half-and-half in a shallow bowl, whisking slightly to break up the eggs. Soak the sliced bread in the egg mixture. Melt the butter in a large nonstick sauté pan or skillet over medium-high heat. Fry the soaked bread slices in the butter until deep golden brown on both sides. Lift with tongs and place on the wire rack. Mix the cinnamon, nutmeg, and sugar and dust over the bread. Set aside and keep warm.

Prepare the sauce. Melt the butter, brown sugar, cinnamon, and nutmeg in a small sauté pan or skillet over medium heat. When bubbling hot, add the liqueur and rum, avert your face and carefully ignite with a match; shake the pan until the alcohol is burned off and the flame dies down. Add the banana slices and toss until coated. Set aside; keep warm.

To serve, spread 1 tablespoon of the sauce in the center of each plate. Lay 2 pieces of French toast on top of the sauce. Form quenelles of the ice cream and place 2 on top of the French toast on each plate. Spoon sauce and bananas over the ice cream and French toast. Garnish each plate with candied walnuts and a sprig of mint, dust with confectioners sugar.

FOR THE BANANAS FOSTER SAUCE:

1 cup (2 sticks) unsalted butter

2 cups light brown sugar

2 teaspoons cinnamon

½ teaspoon nutmeg

½ ounce banana liqueur

2 ounces light rum

2 bananas, peeled and sliced into thin disks

TO SERVE:

1 quart vanilla bean ice cream

4 sprigs mint, for garnish

Confectioners sugar, for dusting

AMELIA BROUSSARD, *LOUISIANA MORNING,* OIL AND ACRYLIC

Lafayette ★

FOR THE BREAD PUDDING:

3 to 4 loaves French bread, torn or cut into small pieces

6 eggs, beaten

4 cups milk

2 cups evaporated milk

2 cups sugar

2 teaspoons ground cinnamon

2 teaspoons ground nutmeg

2 teaspoons pure vanilla extract

½ cup (1 stick) butter, melted

½ cup (1 stick) cold butter, chopped

FOR THE JACK DANIEL'S SAUCE:

1 cup sugar

½ cup (1 stick) butter

2 to 4 ounces Jack Daniel's whiskey

PREJEAN'S BREAD PUDDING
PREJEAN'S RESTAURANT
ERNEST PREJEAN, CHEF DE CUISINE

In 1980, Robert Guilbeau and his friends built Prejean's Restaurant on farmland passed down to him from his grandparents, Walter and Inez Prejean. Guilbeau wanted to combine the joie de vivre of south Louisiana with the comforts of his grandparents' kitchen. Long before "Cajun" would become a household word, Prejean's was serving those delicious boiled shellfish, gumbos, étouffée, and sauce piquantes the world would come to know and love.

Preheat the oven to 400°F. Place the bread pieces in a large mixing bowl. In another bowl, combine the eggs, milk, evaporated milk, sugar, cinnamon, nutmeg, and vanilla and blend well. Stir in the melted butter.

Add the egg mixture to the bread in bowl and stir until mixed. Let stand until liquid is absorbed and bread is saturated. Pour into a greased 9 x 13 inch pan. Sprinkle chopped butter on top.

Bake 30 minutes. Reduce heat to 350°F and bake 45 to 60 minutes or until center is firm. Remove from heat and serve warm with Jack Daniel's sauce.

JACK DANIEL'S SAUCE

In a saucepan over high heat, combine the sugar with 1 cup of water to make a simple syrup. Add the butter and stir until completely blended. Just prior to serving, add whiskey and serve warm over Prejean's Bread Pudding.

CHERRIES JUBILEE AND WHITE CHOCOLATE BREAD PUDDING

SOBOU RESTAURANT
JUAN CARLOS GONZALEZ, EXECUTIVE CHEF

SoBou stands for South of Bourbon and a modern, small plates approach to traditional New Orleans fare. SoBou is a cocktail-focused restaurant with an extensive happy hour menu. Note that this is best prepared a day before serving.

In a large bowl, whisk together the cream, eggs, vanilla extract, cinnamon, and nutmeg. While still whisking, gradually pour in the sugar and continue mixing until it is dissolved. Add the cubed French bread and mix by hand; add the cherries and chocolate and mix by hand. For best results, refrigerate overnight.

Preheat the oven to 300°F.

Scoop 1 cup of the bread pudding into small baking ramekins, top with 5 chocolate coins and 5 cherries. Bake for 15 to 20 minutes, or until the center is "mushy" but not "milky" and the top is golden brown. Garnish with candied pecans, if using, and powdered sugar. Serve with a scoop of vanilla ice cream.

New Orleans ★

SERVES 6

1 quart heavy cream

8 eggs

1 tablespoon pure vanilla extract

1 tablespoon ground cinnamon

Pinch of ground nutmeg

1 cup sugar

4 to 5 cups stale French bread, cubed

1½ cups brandied cherries, strained from liquid (plus 30 more for garnish)

1½ cups white chocolate coins (plus 30 more for garnish)

2 cups candied pecans, optional

Powdered sugar, for garnish

Vanilla ice cream, for serving

A PRECURSOR TO BREAD PUDDING, thrifty Old-World French cooks used stale bread to create the classic dessert known as *pain perdu* (or "lost bread"). Thanks to its French heritage and its excellent bread, New Orleans might be called the bread pudding capital of the world—certainly the city has made this luxurious dessert its own. Many Louisiana restaurants and a good number of home cooks are justly famous for their unique recipe.

Alexandria ★

SERVES 6

FOR THE PUDDING:

18 large glazed donuts
or 25 slices good-quality
white bread

1 quart half-and-half

½ cup sugar (see Note)

1 tablespoon pure vanilla
extract

4 (12-ounce) bags white
chocolate chips

8 large eggs

**FOR THE WHITE
CHOCOLATE SAUCE:**

1 cup heavy whipping
cream

2 (12-ounce) bags white
chocolate chips

ROY'S FAMOUS WHITE CHOCOLATE BREAD PUDDING
CAJUN LANDING
ROY ABSHIRE, CHEF

Cajun Landing takes bread pudding up a notch by using glazed donuts as a base. You could substitute good white bread for the donuts, but where's the fun in that?

Preheat the oven to 350°F. Cut the donuts into cubes and place into a large bowl.

In a saucepan, heat the half-and-half then remove from the heat. Add the white chocolate chips, sugar, and vanilla. Stir until the chips are melted. In a separate bowl, whisk the eggs then slowly stir them into the chocolate mixture until well combined.

Pour the chocolate mixture into the bowl of donuts. Mix gently, taking care not to mash the donuts—they should still be in visible cubes once mixed.

Pour into a greased pan and bake for about 1 hour, or until the bread pudding puffs up and turns golden brown. Serve hot with white chocolate sauce.

Note: If using bread instead of donuts, increase sugar to 1 cup.

WHITE CHOCOLATE SAUCE
Heat the cream in a pot placed over low flame. Remove from the heat, add the white chocolate chips, and stir until melted. Serve hot.

WHITE CHOCOLATE BISCUIT PUDDING
CAFÉ ADELAIDE
CARL SCHAUBHUT, EXECUTIVE CHEF

New Orleans

Inspired by Adelaide Brennan, beloved aunt of the youngest generation of Brennan family restaurateurs, Café Adelaide serves a Creole menu centered highlighting the cocktails served at their Swizzle Stick Bar. Buttermilk biscuits are the centerpiece of this white chocolate bread pudding.

In a large bowl, mix the eggs, heavy cream, milk, butter, sugar, vanilla, and cinnamon until well combined. Add chocolate and broken up biscuits to the custard and allow to set for 20 to 30 minute.

Preheat oven to 325°F. Transfer the biscuit pudding to individual ramekins or a baking dish and bake for about 25 minutes. Garnish warm pudding with chopped nuts and white chocolate then finish with warm root beer syrup and a scoop of ice cream.

ROOT BEER SYRUP

Combine the root beer and corn syrup in a small saucepan and reduce by half over medium heat. Reserve and hold warm.

SERVES 8

FOR THE BISCUIT PUDDING:

4 eggs

2 cups heavy cream

1 cup milk

½ cup (1 stick) butter, melted

1 cup sugar

1 teaspoon pure vanilla extract

½ teaspoon cinnamon

½ cup chopped white chocolate

8 buttermilk biscuits

FOR THE ROOT BEER SYRUP:

2 (12-ounce) bottles Abita root beer, or your favorite brand

2 cups light corn syrup

Chopped white chocolate, for garnish

Chopped toasted pecans, for garnish

White chocolate ice cream, for serving

New Orleans ★

SERVES 6

FOR THE FILLING:

7 ounces (½ package) dried Kalamata figs

1 ounce Benedictine liqueur

1 ounce brandy

4 bananas, preferably over-ripe, peeled and sliced

Sugar, to taste

1 cup toasted pecans

FOR THE BISCUITS:

1 cup all-purpose flour

⅓ teaspoon salt

1 teaspoon baking powder

1 tablespoon sugar

⅓ cup butter

⅓ cup buttermilk

Caramel sauce, for serving

Ice cream, for serving

FIG BENEDICTINE BANANA COBBLER
COMMANDER'S PALACE
TORY MCPHAIL, EXECUTIVE CHEF

This sophisticated version of a classic cobbler would be the perfect ending to a holiday meal. Adjust the amount of sugar used in the filling according to the sweetness of the figs.

Make the filling. Slice the figs in half and place in a saucepan over medium heat. Cover with water to reconstitute until soft. Be careful—they will absorb a lot more water than you think, and will definitely stick and burn if left unattended.

When the figs are soft, drain any liquid, and deglaze the pan with the brandy and Benedictine. Add sliced bananas and cook until very soft. Fold in the roasted pecans and sweeten with sugar to taste. Spread this mixture on a sheet pan to cool.

Make the biscuits. Preheat the oven to 350°F. Sift together the flour, salt, baking powder, and sugar. Cut the butter into dime-sized pieces and gently mix with the dry ingredients. Don't break the butter up too much.

Form a well in the center of the mixture and pour in the buttermilk. Lightly mix. It should be sticky; if not, add more buttermilk.

Pat the dough out to ½-inch thick on a buttered and floured baking sheet. Bake halfway (still not brown or dry). Remove from the oven and use a spatula to chop the dough into small pieces.

Butter and flour six 10-ounce ceramic ramekins. Line the bottoms of the ramekins with a ¼-inch layer of biscuit crumbs. Follow with a ½-inch layer of fig filling. Repeat this step, topping with a third layer of crumb.

Bake until brown and bubbly. Allow to cool almost completely, run the rim with a paring knife, and turn out onto a plate. Serve with a caramel sauce and your favorite ice cream.

HUI JIN, *CAFÉ DU MONDE*, OIL AND ACRYLIC

★
Bossier City

SERVES 8

FOR THE CRUST:

1 cup graham cracker crumbs

½ cup sugar

3 tablespoons butter, melted

FOR THE FILLING:

1 cup sugar

1 tablespoon pure vanilla extract

4 (8-ounce) packages cream cheese, softened

½ cup sour cream

6 tablespoons butter, melted

2 eggs

12 ounces chocolate chips

FOR THE TEA:

1 gallon brewed tea

1 ½ cups sugar

2 orange slices

2 lemon slices

2 ounces orange juice

2 ounces lemon juice

6 mint leaves, torn into pieces (do not cut)

Orange and lemon wedges, for serving

NOTINI'S FROZEN CHEESECAKE
NOTINI'S
STANLEY, RONNIE, AND JERRY NOTINI KOLNIAK, OWNERS

This family-run casual Italian restaurant is authentic right down to its red-checkered tablecloths. Fans travel for miles for the house-made marina sauce (also sold in jars on the premises) and the muffalettas. Another specialty of the house is the cheesecake, which is served frozen. Note that this cake should be made at least 24 hours before serving.

Preheat the oven to 350°F.

Make the filling. Add the sugar and vanilla to the bowl of a stand mixer fitted with the paddle attachment. Mix at low speed for 3 minutes. Add the cream cheese and mix for 5 minutes, boosting speed to medium after 2 minutes. Add the sour cream and mix for 3 minutes. Add the melted butter and mix for 3 minutes more. Beat the eggs and add, mix for 5 minutes more, until the filling is uniform. Fold in three-quarters of the chocolate chips, reserving the rest.

Make the crust. In a small bowl, mix together the graham cracker crumbs, sugar, and melted butter. Press the mixture into a 9-inch, greased spring-form pan.

Pour the filling over the crust, top with remaining chocolate chips and bake for 50 minutes. Let the cheesecake cool on a wire rack in the pan. When cool, place the cake—in its pan— directly into freezer for 24 hours. The next day, remove the cake from the pan and return it to the freezer until ready to serve. Cut frozen.

NOTINI'S MINT SPICED TEA

Notini's customers are passionate about this refreshing tea—it's so popular, the restaurant sells it by the gallon.

In a large pitcher, mix the tea, sugar, orange and lemon slices, orange and lemon juice, and mint. Chill, and serve in a glass garnished with orange and lemon wedges.

SATSUMA CREOLE CREAM-CHEESE CHEESECAKE

DICKIE BRENNAN'S BOURBON HOUSE
DARIN NESBIT, EXECUTIVE CHEF

New Orleans ★

SERVES 8

Dickie Brennan's devotion to seasonal food extends to the dessert menu with this cheesecake flavored with satsuma oranges. This seedless mandarin is found in tropical climates around the world, but in the United States, its primary habitat is southern Louisiana.

Make the crust. In a mixing bowl, combine the graham cracker crumbs, sugar, and melted butter. Press into a 9 x 3-inch spring-form pan. Refrigerate until ready to fill.

Make the filling. Preheat the oven to 250°F. In the bowl of a stand mixer with a paddle attachment combine the cream cheese and sugar. Mix until smooth, occasionally scraping down the sides with a spatula. Add the Creole cream cheese, zest and juice, and mix until smooth. Add one egg at a time, scraping the sides of the bowl with a spatula. Mix well after each egg.

Pour the batter into the prepared crust and bake for two hours, until the center of the cake is firm to the touch. Let cool at room temperature before refrigerating until ready to serve.

Make the compote. Peel and segment the satsumas, reserving any juice (supplement with orange juice as needed). Heat the juice, sugar and cinnamon stick in a saucepan over medium heat and bring to a boil. Reduce heat and simmer until the liquid becomes syrupy, approximately 20 minutes. Remove cinnamon stick and fold in satsuma segments and berries (strawberries should be quartered). Add Grand Marnier and serve over the cheesecake.

Note: Creole cream cheese is a farmer's cheese found primarily in New Orleans and elsewhere in Louisiana. Similar to sour cream and yogurt, it is made from skim milk, buttermilk, and rennet.

FOR THE CRUST

2 cups graham cracker crumbs

½ cup sugar

½ cup (1 stick) butter, melted

FOR THE FILLING:

5 (8-ounce) packages cream cheese, softened

1¼ cups sugar

1¼ cups Creole cream cheese (see Note), or sour cream

2 teaspoons satsuma zest

¼ cup satsuma juice

3 medium eggs

FOR THE SATSUMA COMPOTE

6 satsumas

½ cup satsuma or orange juice

3 tablespoons sugar

1 cinnamon stick

1 pint Louisiana strawberries, blackberries, or raspberries

1 ounce Grand Marnier liqueur

Lafayette
★

FOR THE CRUST:

2 cups graham cracker crumbs

½ cup sugar

½ cup (1 stick) butter, melted

FOR THE FILLING:

4 (8-ounce) packages cream cheese, softened

8 ounces creamy peanut butter, softened

1¼ cups sugar

1¼ cups Creole cream cheese, John Folse Bittersweet Plantation brand preferred (see Note)

3 eggs

FOR THE CANDIED BACON:

10 slices good-quality smoked bacon

1 cup sugar

FOR THE BERRY COM-POTE:

4 cups blueberries

4 cups raspberries

4 cups sliced strawberries

2 cups sugar

GRACELAND
BLUE DOG CAFÉ
STEVE SANTILLO/ANDRE RODRIGUE, OWNERS

Here is a delicious tribute to the King: a peanut-butter cheesecake with caramelized bananas, three-berry compote, and candied bacon. As Elvis would say: thank you, thank you very much! Note that this cake is made one day before serving.

Make the crust. Combine the graham cracker crumbs, sugar, and butter. Mix thoroughly and press evenly over the bottom and sides of a 9-inch spring-form pan. Refrigerate for at least 30 minutes.

Make the filling. Preheat the oven to 250°F. In the bowl of a stand mixer with the paddle attachment, cream together the regular cream cheese, peanut butter, and sugar. Mix until smooth, occasionally scraping the bowl with a spatula. Add the Creole cream cheese and mix until smooth. Add the eggs one at a time, and mix until smooth after each addition. Pour the batter into the chilled crust and bake for 2 hours, or until the center is set. Let the cake cool then refrigerate overnight, until completely chilled.

Make the candied bacon. Preheat the oven to 400°F. Spread the bacon flat over a parchment-lined cookie sheet and sprinkle generously with sugar. Bake until brown and crispy, 10 to 15 minutes. (Be especially watchful as sugar may easily burn in oven hot spots and tray may have to be rotated periodically.) Let cool and set aside.

Make the berry compote. Combine the blueberries, raspberries, strawberries, sugar, and 2 cups of water in medium saucepan over medium heat. Let the mixture cook down until it coats the back of a spoon. Allow to cool and set aside.

Make the banana topping. Cover the cooled cheesecake with sliced bananas and sprinkle the sugar over the bananas. Lightly caramelize sugar with a kitchen torch, being careful not to melt cheesecake below. Allow banana topping to cool as well.

After the topping has cooled, run a knife between the sides of the pan and the crust and then release the sides of the spring-form pan. Cut the cake into equal pieces using a long knife that has been dipped in hot water between every cut. Drizzle with the berry compote and garnish with candied bacon.

Note: Creole cream cheese is a farmer's cheese found primarily in New Orleans and elsewhere in Louisiana. Similar to sour cream and yogurt, it is made from skim milk, buttermilk, and rennet. Sour cream is a good substitute.

FOR TOPPING:

4 ripe bananas, sliced

1 cup sugar

JESSI STACK, *DONUT INSPECTOR*, OIL AND ACRYLIC

DARK CHOCOLATE SWEET-POTATO PECAN PIE
CHARLEY G'S
HOLLY GOETTING, EXECUTIVE CHEF

Lafayette ★

This is a seasonal take on the pecan pie that is always on the restaurant's dessert menu. For an even more decadent dessert, Chef Goetting suggests serving with your favorite ice cream. To save time, a pre-made pie crust can be used.

Make the crust. Preheat the oven to 350°F. Roll out the pie dough on a lightly floured surface to fill a deep-dish, 9-inch pie pan. Fit the dough inside the pan, fill with the pecans and chocolate, and set aside.

Make the filling. In a large mixing bowl, combine the sugar and flour and mix. Beat in the eggs and yolks, then add the corn syrup, vanilla, Frangelico, evaporated milk, and salt. Stir to blend, then stir in the sweet potato puree.

Pour into the pie shell and bake until filling is set and the pastry is golden brown, 45 minutes to an hour.

SWEET PIE DOUGH
In the bowl of a stand mixer with paddle attachment mix the butter and sugar until incorporated. Then add in the egg, yolk, and flour. Mix until well blended. Form the dough into a disk and refrigerate for 30 minutes.

SERVES 8

1 prepared sweet pie dough crust

1¼ cups pecan pieces

4 ounces dark chocolate, chopped

1 cup sugar

2 tablespoons flour

3 eggs

2 egg yolks

1 cup corn syrup

1 teaspoon pure vanilla extract

2 ounces Frangelico liqueur

4 ounces evaporated milk

1 teaspoon salt

4 ounces canned sweet potato pie puree

FOR THE PIE DOUGH:

1 pound (4 sticks) butter, cold

½ pound sugar

1 egg

1 egg yolk

1½ pounds all-purpose flour

CARRIE WILLIAMSON, *PECAN PIE,* PENCIL AND GRAPHITE (DETAIL)

New Orleans ★

SERVES 8

FOR THE MOUSSE:

1 pint fresh blackberries

1¼ cups sugar

12 egg yolks

9 egg whites

14 ounces bittersweet chocolate, chopped

4 cups heavy cream

FOR THE PHYLLO CRISPS:

8 sheets phyllo dough

1 cup (2 sticks) butter, melted

½ cup sugar

½ tablespoon cinnamon

½ tablespoon freshly grated nutmeg

FOR THE WHITE CHOCOLATE GANACHE:

3 cups heavy cream

16 ounces white chocolate, chopped

BITTERSWEET CHOCOLATE–BLACKBERRY MOUSSE NAPOLEON
COMMANDER'S PALACE
TORY MCPHAIL, EXECUTIVE CHEF

A sophisticated dessert from one of New Orleans best-known restaurants. Feel free to substitute other berries if blackberries are out of season.

Make the mousse. Puree the blackberries in a blender and strain through a fine-mesh sieve. In the top of a double boiler, combine the blackberry liquid, ½ of the sugar, and the egg yolks. Heat the mixture, whipping constantly to prevent over-heating. The egg yolks should come to a ribbon consistency, about 145°F.

Whip the egg whites separately, gradually adding the remaining sugar until stiff.

Melt the chocolate in a double boiler, remove from heat, and add the egg-yolk mixture. Fold a small portion of the whipped egg whites into the chocolate-egg yolk mixture using a rubber spatula. Fold the remaining whites into the mixture and set aside in the refrigerator.

Whip the cream to stiff peaks. Fold into the chocolate mixture with rubber spatula. Chill for 2 hours.

Make the phyllo crisps. Preheat the oven to 300°F. Put 2 sheets of phyllo dough down on the work surface, slightly overlapping on one. Brush with the melted butter. Place 2 more sheets on the butter-moistened dough and brush tops. Repeat procedure until you have 4 layers.

Brush the top with butter one more time, mix the sugar, cinnamon, and nutmeg and sprinkle liberally on top of the phyllo stacks. Cut in triangles with 2-inch sides. Bake on a baking sheet between 2 pieces of parchment until golden brown, about 15 minutes. Set aside.

KATIE MURPHY, *BLUEPLATE SPECIAL,* OIL AND ACRYLIC

Make the ganache. Bring the cream to a boil. Put the chocolate in a heat-proof container and pour the hot cream over it. Stir until the chocolate has all melted. Keep warm.

Make the blackberry coulis. Puree blackberries in a blender and strain. Pour the juice in a non-reactive pan and bring it to a simmer. Add the sugar. Make a slurry with the cornstarch and ½ cup water. Stir the slurry into the juice and return to simmer to thicken. Let cool.

To serve, place dollop (about 2 tablespoons) of the mousse in the center of the plate. Place one of baked phyllo triangles on top and gently press flat. Repeat 2 more times to complete 3 layers. Using a spoon, drizzle the ganache and the coulis around the Napoleon. Garnish with fresh blackberries.

FOR THE BLACKBERRY COULIS:

1 pint fresh blackberries

¾ cup sugar

½ cup cornstarch

Fresh blackberries, for garnish

Lafayette
★

SERVES 4

FOR THE SHORTBREAD:

4 cups all-purpose flour

2½ cups sugar

½ cup ground Szechuan peppercorns

Pinch of salt

1¾ cups (3½ sticks) unsalted butter, diced into small cubes

4 egg yolks

FOR THE BERRY-CHAMPAGNE COMPOTE:

3 cups frozen strawberries

1 cup Champagne, or sparkling wine

2 cups sugar

Pinch of salt

1 cup frozen blueberries

Vanilla ice cream, for serving

4 sprigs thyme, for garnish

SZECHUAN SHORTBREAD WITH VANILLA ICE CREAM
THE FRENCH PRESS
JUSTIN GIROUARD, CO-OWNER/CHEF

This intimate restaurant, housed in a former printing plant, goes casual for breakfast and lunch during the week, then pulls out the white tablecloths for Friday and Saturday night dining, mixing Cajun and French cuisines with Southern favorites. A native of Lafayette, James Beard–nominee Chef Girourd's inventiveness is shown in this shortbread, spiced with Szechuan pepper, and served with ice cream and a berry-Champagne compote.

Make the shortbread. Preheat the oven to 350°F. In a large mixing bowl, combine the flour, sugar, ground peppercorns, and salt and mix well. Add the butter and with your hands work it into the dry mixture until the size of peas. Add the egg yolks and mix until combined, being careful not to overwork the dough.

Using a rolling pin roll the dough out on a silicone baking sheet to a consistent thickness of ½ inch.

Bake for 20 minutes, rotate, and finish for another 20 minutes, or until golden brown but still soft in the middle (like a giant sugar cookie.)

Make the compote. In a large saucepan, combine the strawberries, Champagne, sugar, and salt. Bring to a simmer and cook, stirring occasionally, for 30 minutes. Add the blueberries and cook for 20 minutes more, or until it reaches a nice sauce-like consistency.

To serve, crumble the shortbread into medium-sized pieces and place on a baking sheet to warm in the oven. Divide the warmed shortbread crumbles into the bottom of 4 large bowls and ladle the warm compote onto the shortbread. Place a hearty scoop of your favorite vanilla ice cream on top (we make our own at the restaurant). Garnish with a thyme sprig and serve.

PREJEAN'S SWEET LOUISIANA PRALINES
PREJEAN'S RESTAURANT
ERNEST PREJEAN, CHEF DE CUISINE

This sweet confection came to Louisiana with the first French settlers. The American version, with its added milk, is more like fudge than its French counterpart. Prejean's pralines are so popular, they sell them at the restaurant check out.

In a heavy 2-quart saucepan, heat the butter until melted. Blend in both sugars. Cook and stir until the sugar dissolves.

Stir in the cream until blended. Bring mixture to a rolling boil, stirring continuously. Reduce heat to medium high and stir continuously until mixture becomes foamy and frothy, darkens in color, and reaches soft-crack stage. To test for soft-crack stage, between 270° and 290°F on a candy thermometer, drop a small amount into ice water; the drop should form hard but pliable threads.

Remove from heat. Stir in the vanilla and pecans. Continue to stir for 5 minutes or until mixture begins to stiffen. Spoon individual circles of mixture onto waxed paper. Allow pralines to cool completely before removing from waxed paper.

Lafayette ★

MAKES ABOUT SIXTEEN
3-INCH ROUND PRALINES

½ cup (1 stick) butter

1¾ cups sugar

½ pound light brown sugar

2 cups heavy cream

2 tablespoons pure vanilla extract

1 pound pecans

Mandeville ★

MAKES 1 LARGE OR 2 SMALL RINGS

FOR THE FILLING:

½ cup brown sugar

½ cup sugar

1 tablespoon cinnamon

4 tablespoons (½ stick) butter

FOR THE CAKE:

6 cups flour, divided

½ cup sugar, divided

2 packages (4½ teaspoons) dry yeast

⅓ cup very warm water

½ cup (1 stick) butter or margarine, softened

⅔ cup evaporated milk

1 teaspoon salt

4 eggs

1 teaspoon dehydrated lemon zest (or 1 table-spoon fresh), optional

1 teaspoon dehydrated orange zest (or 1 table-spoon fresh), optional

KING CAKE
MANDEVILLE HIGH SCHOOL
CAROLYN SENAC, PROSTART INSTRUCTOR

Instructor Senac uses this recipe, which she adapted from an original bakery recipe, in her classroom. Associated around the world with the Epiphany, when the Magi arrived bearing gifts for the Christ child, King Cake is baked in honor of the three kings. The Epiphany (or Twelfth Night) is also the beginning of Mardi Gras season, and so this colorful cake has become synonymous with Mardi Gras in New Orleans. The colors purple (representing justice), green (faith), and gold (power) are said to have been chosen by Rex in 1872.

Make the filling. In a small bowl, mix together the sugars and cinnamon. Melt the butter in small bowl. Set the 2 bowls aside until needed.

Make the cake. Spoon flour into a dry measuring cup and pour 4 cups onto waxed paper. Keep 1 cup aside. Combine 2 tablespoons of the sugar, yeast, and the very warm water in the bowl of a stand mixer fitted with the paddle attachment. Let it stand till it foams. (Don't make your water too hot or it will kill the yeast.)

Melt the butter in 2-cup measure; add the evaporated milk, the remaining ⅓ cup sugar, and salt. Stir to combine and set aside to cool.

Beat the eggs into the yeast mixture. Add the milk mixture and the zest, if using, and mix well. Continue beating, adding 3 to 3½ cups flour, ½ cup at a time.

Add remaining flour and switch the paddle for the dough hook. Knead the dough, adding the remaining cup of flour if necessary, until the dough is smooth and elastic, 5 to 10 minutes. Turn the dough out onto floured board or counter. Cover with waxed paper, then a dry kitchen towel, and let rest for 1 hour on the counter

Punch down the dough and, using a rolling pin dusted with flour, roll into a 15 x 30-inch rectangle. The dough should be very thin. Cut into 3 strips, lengthwise, to braid. Brush with the melted butter, and sprinkle with cinnamon-sugar mixture.

ALLYSON SUTTON, *WHO'S GOT THE BABY?,* OIL AND ACRYLIC (NINTH PLACE SENIOR)

Braid the 3 strips and make a circle by joining ends. Place on greased baking sheet. Brush the surface of the dough with oil or butter. Cover loosely with plastic wrap. (Alternatively, brush the rectangle of dough with the melted butter and sprinkle the cinnamon-sugar on top. Roll the dough like a jellyroll and form into a circle by joining the ends. Proceed as directed.)

Let the cake rise, covered, in a warm place until doubled in size. (The cake can be refrigerated at this point for 2 to 24 hours. When ready to bake remove from the refrigerator, un-cover, and let stand for 20 minutes before baking.)

Preheat the oven to 350°F. Bake for 20 to 25 minutes, or until golden brown. Remove to cooling rack and cool for 20 minutes.

Make the icing. In a small bowl, mix the powdered sugar and lemon juice until smooth. The mixture should be thick. If us-ing food coloring, divide into 3 bowls and tint to desired shade.

Drizzle the icing on the cooled cake and decorate with colored sugar.

FOR THE ICING:

1½ cups powdered sugar

1 tablespoon lemon juice or milk

Food coloring (purple, green, and gold), optional

Colored sugar (purple, green, and gold), for sprinkling

LIST OF PARTICIPATING RESTAURANTS

The Louisiana Restaurant Association Education Foundation and the George Rodrigue Foundation of the Arts are grateful to the following restaurants for their generosity in providing the recipes in this book.

THE AMERICAN SECTOR
A JOHN BESH RESTAURANT
AT THE NATIONAL WWII MUSEUM
945 Magazine Street
New Orleans, LA 70130
(504) 528-1940
www.nationalww2museum.org
www.chefjohnbesh.com

ANDREA'S NEW ORLEANS ITALIAN RESTAURANT
3100 19th Street at Ridgelake
Metairie, LA 70002
(504) 834-8583
www.andreasrestaurant.com

ARNAUD'S
813 Rue Bienville
New Orleans, LA 70112
(504) 523-5433
www.arnaudsrestaurant.com

BACCO ITALIAN GRILLE
300 Washington Street
Monroe, LA 71201
(318) 737-7578

BAYONA
430 Dauphine Street
New Orleans, LA 70122
(504) 525-4455
www.bayona.com

BELLA FRESCA
6307 Line Avenue
Shreveport, LA 71106
(318) 865-6307
www.bellafresca.com

BLUE DOG CAFÉ
1211 West Pinhook Road
Lafayette, LA 70503
(337) 237-0005
www.bluedogcafe.com

BORGNE
A John Besh Restaurant
601 Loyola Avenue
New Orleans, LA 70113
(504) 613-3860
www.borgnerestaurant.com

BRIGTSEN'S RESTAURANT
723 Dante Street
New Orleans, LA 70118
(504) 861-7610
www.brigtsens.com

CAFÉ ADELAIDE
300 Poydras Street
New Orleans, LA 70130
(504) 595-3305
www.cafeadelaide.com

CAFÉ B RESTAURANT
BY RALPH BRENNAN
2700 Metairie Road
Metairie, LA 70001
(504) 934-4700
www.cafeb.com

CAFÉ DOMINIQUE
8013 Main Street
Houma, LA 70360
(985) 223-7540
www.cafedominique.com

CAJUN LANDING
2728 N. MacArthur Drive
Alexandria, LA 71303
(318) 487-4912
www.cajunlanding.com

CHARLEY G'S
3809 Ambassador Caffery Parkway
Lafayette, LA 70503
(337) 981-0108
www.charleygs.com

CLEMENTINE RESTAURANT
113 East Main Street
New Iberia, LA 70560
(337) 560-1007
www.clementinedowntown.com

COMMANDER'S PALACE
1403 Washington Avenue
New Orleans, LA 70130
(504) 899-8221
www.commanderspalace.com

COTTON
101 North Grand Street
Monroe, LA 71201
(318) 325-0818
www.restaurantcotton.com

DICKIE BRENNAN'S BOURBON HOUSE
144 Bourbon Street
New Orleans, LA 70130
(504) 522-0111
www.bourbonhouse.com

DICKIE BRENNAN'S PALACE CAFÉ
605 Canal Street
New Orleans, LA 70130
(504) 523-1661
www.palacecafe.com

DICKIE BRENNAN'S STEAKHOUSE
716 Iberville Street
New Orlenas, LA 70130
(504) 522-2467
www.dickiebrennanssteakhouse.com

DOMENICA RESTAURANT
123 Baronne Street
New Orleans, LA 70112
(504) 648-6020
www.domenicarestaurant.com

DON'S SEAFOOD
6823 Airline Highway
Baton Rouge, LA 70805
(225) 357-0601
www.donsseafoodonline.com

DRAGO'S SEAFOOD RESTAURANT
2 Poydras Street
New Orleans, LA 70130
(504) 584-3911
3232 North Arnoult Road
Metairie, LA 70002
(504) 888-9254
www.dragosrestaurant.com

DOOKY CHASE'S RESTAURANT
2301 Orleans Avenue
New Orleans, LA 70119
(504) 821-0600
www.dookychaserestaurant.com

EMERIL'S NEW ORLEANS
800 Tchoupitoulas Street
New Orleans, LA 70130
(504) 528-9393
www.emerilsrestaurants.com

**ERNEST'S ORLEANS RESTAURANT
AND COCKTAIL LOUNGE**
1601 Spring Street
Shreveport, LA 71101
(318) 226-1325
www.ernestsorleans.com

FLANAGAN'S
1111 Audubon Avenue
Thibodaux, LA 70301
(985) 447-7771
www.fremins.net

THE FRENCH PRESS
214 East Vermilion Street
Lafayette, LA 70501
(337) 233-9449
www.thefrenchpresslafayette.com

GALATOIRE'S
209 Bourbon Street
New Orleans, LA 70130
(504) 525-2021
www.galatoires.com

GALATOIRE'S BISTRO
3535 Perkins Road, Suite 400
Baton Rouge, lA
(225) 753-4864
www.galatoiresbistro.com

GW FINS
808 Bienville Street
New Orleans, LA 70112
(504) 581-3467
www.gwfins.com

HERITAGE GRILL BY RALPH BRENNAN
111 Veterans Memorial Blvd
Metairie, LA 70005
(504) 934-4900
www.heritagegrillmetairie.com

LATIL'S LANDING RESTAURANT
AT HOUMAS HOUSE PLANTATION
AND GARDENS
40136 Louisiana 942
Darrow, LA 70725
(225) 473-9380
www.houmashouse.com

HOUSE OF BLUES NEW ORLEANS
225 Decatur Street
New Orleans, LA 70130
(504) 310-4999
www.houseofblues.com/NewOrleans

JACK DEMPSEY'S RESTAURANT
738 Poland Avenue
New Orleans, LA 70117
(504) 943-9914
www.jackdempseys.net

JOLIE'S LOUISIANA BISTRO
507 W. Pinhook Road
Lafayette, LA 70503
(337) 706-8544
www.jolieslouisianabistro.com

JUBAN'S
3739 Perkins Road
Baton Rouge, LA 70808
(225) 346-8422
www.jubans.com

K-PAUL'S LOUISIANA KITCHEN
416 Chartres Street
New Orleans, LA 70130
(504) 596-2530
www.chefpaul.com

LA PROVENCE
A CHEF JOHN BESH RESTAURANT
25020 Highway 190
Lacombe, LA 70445
(985) 626-7662
www.laprovencerestaurant.com

LA TRUFFE SAUVAGE
815 W. Bayou Pines Drive
Lake Charles, LA 70601
(337) 439-8364
www.thewildtruffle.com

LE MOYNE DE BIENVILLE CLUB
666 Gravier Street
New Orleans, LA 70130
(504) 524-4821

LOLA
517 North New Hampshire Street
Covington, LA 70433
(985) 892-4992
www.lolacovington.com

MANSUR'S ON THE BOULEVARD
5720 Corporate Blvd #A
Baton Rouge, LA 70808
(225) 923-3366
www.mansursontheboulevard.com

MESTIZO RESTAURANT
2323 Acadian Thruway
Baton Rouge, LA 70806
(225) 387-2699
www.mestizorestaurant.com

MIKE ANDERSON'S SEAFOOD
1031 West Lee Drive
Baton Rouge, LA 70809
(225) 766-7823
www.mikeandersons.com

MOPHO
514 City Park Avenue
New Orleans, LA 70119
www.mophomidcity.com

MR. B'S BISTRO
201 Royal Street
New Orleans, LA 70130
(504) 523-2078
www.mrbsbistro.com

NEW ORLEANS COUNTRY CLUB
5024 Pontchartrain Boulevard
New Orleans, LA 70118
(504) 482-2145
www.neworleanscountryclub.com

NICHOLAS CATERING
345 Highway 307, Lot 1
Thibodaux, LA 70301
(985) 633-9404
www.nicholascatering.com

NOTINI'S
2013-A Airline Drive
Bossier City, LA 71111
(318) 742-6660
www.notinis.net

PAMPLONA TAPAS BAR AND RESTAURANT
631 Jefferson Street
Lafayette, LA 70501
(337) 232-0070
www.pamplonatapas.com

PÊCHE
800 Magazine Street
New Orleans, LA 70130
(504) 522-1744
www.pecherestaurant.com

POPPY'S THE CRAZY LOBSTER
BAR & GRILL
500 Port of New Orleans Place
Suite 83
New Orleans, La 70130
(504) 569-3380
www.thecrazylobster.com

PREJEAN'S RESTAURANT
3480 NE Evangeline Thruway
Lafayette, LA 70507
(337) 896-3247
www.prejeans.com

RAISING CANE'S (#1)
3313 Highland Road
Baton Rouge, LA 70802
(225) 387-3533
www.raisingcanes.com

RALPH'S ON THE PARK
900 City Park Avenue
New Orleans, LA 70119
(504) 488-1000
www.ralphsonthepark.com

RALPH BRENNAN'S CAFÉ NOMA
*INSIDE THE NEW ORLEANS MUSEUM
OF ART*
#1 Collins Diboll Circle, City Park
New Orleans, LA 70124
(504) 482-1264
www.cafenoma.com

RALPH BRENNAN'S RED FISH GRILL
115 Bourbon Street
New Orleans, LA 70130
(504) 598-1200
www.redfishgrill.com

RESTAURANT AUGUST
A CHEF JOHN BESH RESTAURANT
301 Tchoupitoulas Street
New Orleans, LA 70130
(504) 299-9777
www.restaurantaugust.com

RESTAURANT R'EVOLUTION
777 Bienville Street
New Orleans, LA 70130
(504) 553-2277
www.revolutionnola.com

RESTAURANT STANLEY
547 Saint Ann Street
New Orleans, LA 70116
(504) 587-0093
www.stanleyrestaurant.com

RISTORANTE GIUSEPPE
4800 Line Avenue
Shreveport, LA 71106
(318) 869-4548
www.ristorantegiuseppe.com

ROOT
200 Julia Street
New Orleans, LA 70130
(504) 252-9480
www.rootnola.com

RUFFINO'S
18811 Highland Road
Baton Rouge, LA 70809
(225) 753-3458
www.ruffinosrestaurant.com

RUTH'S CHRIS STEAK HOUSE
525 Fulton Street
New Orleans, LA 70130
(504) 587-7099
3633 Veterans Boulevard
Metaire, LA 70002
(504) 888-3600
www.ruthschris.com

SERENDIPITY
3700 Orleans Avenue
New Orleans, LA 70119
(504) 407-0818
www.serendipitynola.com

THE SHREVEPORT CLUB
410 Travis Street
Shreveport, LA 71101
(318) 221-0618
www.theshreveportclub.com

SLAP YA MAMA
Walker & Sons Inc.
1679 West Main Street
Ville Platte, LA 70586
(800) 485-5217
www.slapyamama.com

SOBOU
310 Chartres Street
New Orleans, LA 70130
(504) 552-4095
www.sobounola.com

STROUBES SEAFOOD AND STEAKS
107 Third Street
Baton Rouge, LA 70801
(225) 448-2830
www.stroubes.com

TSUNAMI
412 Jefferson Street
Lafayette, LA 70501
(337) 234-3474
www.servingsushi.com

WATERFRONT GRILL
5201 DeSiard Street
Monroe, LA 71203
(318) 345-0064
www.waterfrontgrill.com

JENNA BARLOW, *UNTITLED,* PENCIL AND GRAPHITE